Introduction 2

INTERMEDIATE LOAN
MAY BE BORROWED FOR ... WEEKS
D1458284
3.2011

Introduction

My own interest in creative writing began when I was 12 years old. I had moved from South Wales to the Midlands and, at my new school, discovered to my horror that I was required to learn French rather than the Welsh I'd been struggling with back home. When my new French teacher discovered that I spoke not a word of that language, she abandoned any attempt to try and school me and told me to go and sit at the back and 'get on with something quietly'.

Shocking! Outrageous! Shouldn't be allowed! Actually that experience changed my life, because here I was forced by circumstances to sit and think – or, rather, to notice thoughts that simply seemed to drift through my mind. There was nothing else to do. I thought back with fondness to the friends I'd left behind and the adventures we'd had. And I became so wrapped up in reminiscence that I hadn't noticed my teacher walking over to me. But suddenly there she was looking down on me and I guessed I was in Big Trouble! She asked me what I was doing and I said, very honestly, 'Daydreaming Miss.' Then she said something quite remarkable in reply…

'Well why don't you write your daydreams down? Then you'll always remember them.'

And that was the moment my writing career began, together with a love of stories and books that continues unabated. And that (so I tell students when I meet them) was also when I began to realize the meaning of the word opportunity.

On reflection I realize that I was able to take the opportunity to write my daydreams down because of the situation I was in. Boredom had caused me to lapse into the mental state where I could notice my own thoughts. The emotional basis of homesickness sustained my interest in those thoughts. When I was encouraged to write, I had no pressure on me to worry about time, neatness, technical accuracy or how well my classmates could write.

Nor was my work going to be judged by a teacher and found wanting. In the midst of an educational environment that even then emphasized 'objective' standards within a competitive ethos, I found a pocket of quietude where I could just get on and enjoy the experience of expressing my ideas.

Learning the craft of such expression *of course* came to include presentational and technical skills. The ability to communicate clearly, accurately and powerfully is itself an important justification for learning about spelling, grammar, syntax and other more formal aspects of writing. But at the heart of it all lies that essential question and that fundamental challenge – How do I turn the thoughts and feelings inside me into words on the page that other people can understand?

This book suggests some techniques that might help towards an answer.

The thinking link

Concept

What's on your mind?

Thinking precedes speaking and writing. This is an obvious thing to say, but it's all too easy to ask students to 'go and think about' a task we've set without giving them clear strategies as to *how* they will think about it.

We all think in many different ways. This is to say we all possess many thinking tools in our mental toolkit, and people show a range of individual variations, sensory preferences, styles and dispositions about how they notice, shape and react to what goes on inside their heads.

This book will concern itself with how students' writing can be improved through a thinking skills agenda. The emphasis will be on engaging boys with writing, but the ideas and techniques work equally well with female students and span a wide age and ability range.

Four points are worth remembering as we begin…

1. Metacognition boosts learning. Metacognition simply means thinking about the thinking we do. Raising students' awareness of their own mental processes will allow them to become more familiar with and confident in the use of their thinking strategies.

2. The brain loves diversity. Concentration and the inward focusing of attention develop more quickly when thinking tasks are varied.

3. Effective thinking occurs more readily when the learning environment combines low stress and increasing creative challenge.

4. There is no 'right way' of thinking. Individual preferences can be exploited as new strategies are encouraged.

The three top tips for developing as a writer? 'Visualize! Visualize! Visualize!'. Authors combine factual research with their imagination to *experience*, and live, the world they want to write about. A great benefit of using a 'thinking agenda' in teaching writing is then applying these ways of thinking across the curriculum.

Application

■ Encourage students to notice their own thoughts. Point out differences in mind-state between, say, their listening carefully to instructions you give and to a story you tell.

■ Discuss relevant terms. What do your students think 'thinking' means? What is daydreaming? Are there different kinds and intensities of daydreams? Why do we call them 'trains of thought'? What does 'losing the thread' as we speak about something mean? How do we have memories? How are thoughts and feelings connected? What is an idea? How does it feel to have a new idea? Why?

■ Read vivid sentences to your group and ask them to notice what's going on in their minds. Here are some examples.

- Brilliant lightning flickered in the sky above the ruined castle perched on a crag.

- Suddenly the little pink pig turned bright purple.

- Glass shattered nearby.

- The running girl caught a glimpse of the horror that was chasing her.

- He realized that something had changed for the worse.

- The boy swallowed the whole teaspoonful of salt in one go.

Concept

Get an attitude

Creative thinking, however it's applied, depends first and foremost on our attitude and not on the amount of knowledge we possess. Greater knowledge plus effective thinking can lead to increased understanding. This in turn encourages more sophisticated thinking.

The major resources we use in thinking are memory and imagination. Each of us carries a 'map of reality' inside our heads. This is our memory – the incredible network of associations we've created to make sense of the world, based on our unique experiences. Imagination is the ability we have to move mentally beyond the here-and-now. We can create an infinite variety of mental structures. To do this we draw constantly upon our map of memory (look at, for example, Guy Claxton's *Hare Brain Tortoise Mind* to learn more about this).

Both memory and imagination are boosted by adopting the creative attitude. When I work with students I tell them this means 'being nosy' (they appreciate that, because most of them already are!). Such nosiness involves noticing what goes on in the world and inside one's own mind, and asking quality questions. The creative attitude is about exploring, being curious, being playful with ideas and being unafraid of them. This gives rise to creative thinking, which incorporates two vital processes…

1. Linking smaller thoughts and ideas to make more complex mental structures.

2. Looking at things in many different ways: taking a multiple perspective on what we think and experience.

Encouraging a creative attitude in students will make their thinking more powerful and their writing more confident and innovative.

> **TIP:**
> Encouraging means 'to give courage to'. There is no better way of doing this than to write something yourself in the classroom, in front of your students.

Application

Use the picture below – or one like it – to encourage the creative attitude of nosiness.

- **Perspective.** Imagine you are witnessing this scene from aboard the ship in the harbour. Describe the scene.

- **Point of view.** Imagine the man with the sword is a murdering pirate. What might he be thinking right now? Imagine he's a 'good guy' whose friend has just been killed by his opponent. What could he be thinking now?

- **Sensory.** Pretend the picture's in colour. What do you see? Hear the sounds. What are they? Smell the harbour. Describe it.

- **Kinesthetic and empathy.** Pretend you're the man in the middle with the sword. What feelings are going through you at this moment?

Concept

Flexibility within a structure

Thinking / writing tasks that are too prescriptive offer little space for creativity. Tasks that are too vague can leave students floundering. Simply asking someone to write a story or a poem is to request something dauntingly vague. Unless clear thinking and writing strategies are learned and practised, students are tempted to 'make it up as they go along' and produce work derived from novels, movies and so on.

Flexibility within a structure is a general and robust strategy that guides us as we challenge our students to explore and develop their writing. We must make sure that the tasks we give students are clearly supported by strategies they can use to complete them effectively, but which leave enough 'creative space' for young writers to have their own ideas. You'll recognize that most of the techniques in this book follow the principle of flexibility within a structure – and go beyond simply offering writing frames: 'thinking frames' are equally important.

Application

- Refer back to the illustration on p7. Suggest that the central figure carries one unique object, something valuable and one dangerous item about his person. What might they be? And what might happen next? Notice that the students have plenty of visual clues to support their speculation.

- Use 'context sentences' to encourage questioning. Such sentences beg many questions and prick our curiosity. Something like 'Jones lay slumped on the sofa' brings out our natural nosiness. What questions would we like to ask about Jones and his (her? its?) situation.

- Look at the diagram below (see also Storylining on p16). This is an example of a technique called 'artful vagueness', where precise information is surrounded by mystery which in turn encourages us to speculate. We know that danger occurs at precisely this point in the story, but what kind of danger and to whom, and how it's resolved, and so on remain vague.

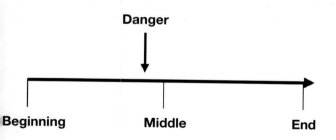

Artful vagueness

Concept

The ownership of language

The concept of 'correct' language often casts a shadow over students' linguistic development. Fear of the wrong answer, whenever it occurs, inhibits the creative exploration of words especially if, as teachers, our emphasis is focused disproportionately on technical accuracy and neatness. Howard Gardner's extensive work in the field of multiple intelligences (see for example *Multiple Intelligences: The Theory in Practice*), informs us that we are born with the potential to become 'linguistically intelligent' – to use language as a life enhancing and life transforming tool. Many factors determine how far that potential is realized including, of course, the richness of the language environment and the child's attitude towards words.

Common sense as well as plenty of research-supported educational theory tells us that a love of language boosts linguistic development. If students are encouraged to feel that language belongs to everyone, and that they own it too, then their willingness to commit themselves to paper will be increased.

Incidentally, have you ever thought about how negative that notion of 'commit' can be? Students are sometimes reluctant to write because they feel they aren't doing it well and that, once on paper, their errors are there for all to see. Help children to enjoy words by encouraging them to boldly go where they might have been nervous to go before!

Application

- Allow students to make networks of associations by raising their awareness of prefixes, suffixes and roots. Whenever possible utilize their words rather than your chosen examples.

- Create etymological word trees (here's an example below) to show relationships and to illustrate that language is liquid. It flows across time and cultures.

- Play with nonsense words whose 'correct' meaning nobody knows. What might these words mean for instance? – *glombous*, *snoodled*, *meshy*, *zxarxz* (see also p38 on synaesthesia). Be aware of how sounds, letter patterns, association / memory and intuition all play a part in making sense of how language works.

- Review the extent to which neatness and technical accuracy act as criteria in your assessment of students' writing. Look at p92 and p94 in this book for broader strategies of assessment.

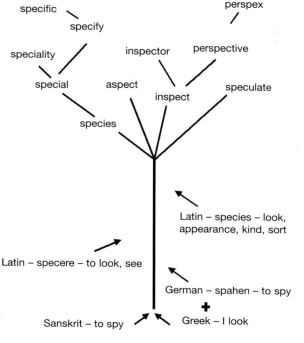

specific
specify
perspex
speciality
inspector
perspective
special
aspect
speculate
inspect
species

Latin – species – look, appearance, kind, sort

Latin – specere – to look, see

German – spahen – to spy
+
Sanskrit – to spy   Greek – I look

Etymological tree

Concept

Strategic thinking:
let's try plan B – and C – and D…

What's the most effective way of teaching students to write well? This is a trick question! Somerset Maugham once told us that 'There are three golden rules for writing successfully – and nobody knows what they are.' Similarly there is no single overall way of allowing the diversity of our students to flourish. So we need to employ strategic thinking.

Strategies work best in the plural. If one particular strategy isn't allowing a student to reach his fixed goal of being a creative and effective writer, then instead of doing that strategy longer and harder, maybe we should try a different one. One of the guiding principles of creativity is that, to have good ideas, we need to have lots of ideas. It's the same with strategies. And if, as teachers, we have enough ideas at our disposal, we should be able to find a way of allowing any and all of our students to progress.

Application

■ Encourage students to notice how they go about preparing to write and how they then endeavour to match their thoughts to words on the page. Have effective writers explain their strategies for doing it well. Use the students as a resource to help build up models of good practice.

■ Be prepared to use all or most of the strategies in this book with your students, even if your own preference selects out just a few. Remember that strategies that you feel comfortable with might not sit easily with some of your students.

■ Show students how decision trees work. This is an effective way of mapping out the thinking – writing – reviewing process. You might consider introducing the technique in the form of a 'story tree' like the one below.

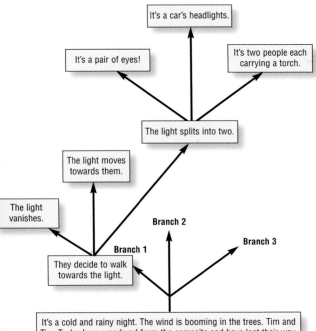

Story tree

Concept

How long does this story have to be?

Minimizing the writing load. That was always my main concern as a boy – how long did the story have to be. The longer it was, the more dismayed I'd become. My teacher's invariable reply was 'Stephen, how long is a piece of string?' which helped me not one bit.

The idea that the more we write, the better we write is but one of many strategies that will work for some students. It's all about experience. And experience is not what happens to us, but what we do with what happens to us.

If students are reluctant, disinterested writers anyway, offering minimal-writing tasks (which maximize thinking, of course!) can make the activity more attractive. Occasionally suggest a maximum number of words for a piece of writing (prose as well as poetry). Always credit the economic use of words.

> **TIP:**
> Emphasize the deliberate choice of words. Encourage students always to 'reach for the right words', the words that express what they are thinking.

Application

- Use writing frames which physically limit the amount that can be written within them. See for example Storylining (p16), Thumbnails (p36), Character cards (p48) and Newspaper articles (p82).

- Use Minisagas as a writing strategy. A minisaga is traditionally a short 'story' of exactly 50 words, plus up to 12 words in the title. Here's an example.

Attack of the Red-Mouthed Edna
I wasn't going to get out of this now. No way. I'd tried everything to stop them from taking me. But here I was trapped, helpless. Parents behind me, door opening ahead. Agh! She's there. That mouth, red, slavering. 'Ooo my lovely boy,' said Aunt Edna. 'Gi's a kiss.' Smack!

- Vary the technique. Ask one group to write first-draft minisagas (these are likely to be over or under 50 words) and another group to edit them to exactly 50 words. Try 'midisagas' of 100 words and 'maxisagas' of 250 words. (One student suggested 'microsagas' of 25 words, but I decided he was just trying to get out of doing some work.)

- Have students plan whole pieces of work but write just the opening and / or closing sections.

- Suggest that in any case 'short and simple' makes for clearer communication than long-winded and elaborate.

Plotting and the big picture

2

Concept

Storylining

Just about every student knows that a story (indeed almost every kind of written form) has a beginning, a middle and an end – although when one boy told me that his stories had a beginning, a muddle and an end I knew exactly what he meant. However, that linear sequence is how the finished project looks. It's a product of the logical-sequential left hemisphere of the neocortex, which is responsible among other things for critical thinking and framing language.

At the earlier stages of the writing process – envisioning and planning – the right hemisphere is busy processing the whole story. This happens largely at a subconscious level, which means that ideas can 'pop up' in any order. The storyline technique illustrated on p9 accommodates the way in which both hemispheres work. The entire 'span' of the work is visually available at a glance, and the line can be annotated at any point as ideas come along. Use the storyline as a planning technique and try out these variations…

Application

■ Start anywhere along the storyline. Have students ask yes-no (closed) questions about what might be happening. Use coin flips (heads = yes / tails = no) to generate random answers.

■ Place simple pictures at points along a storyline and have students work out a linking narrative. Then encourage students to choose pictures of their own to use in the same way.

■ Cut a short story up into separate scenes or paragraphs and ask students to put the cut-ups in the right sequence along a storyline. The storyline technique, incidentally, is an effective way of helping students to remember texts they've studied.

■ Vary the technique by putting physical objects along a line to act as prompts for storymaking. Use stones, shells, leaves, pieces of material, odd items like train tickets, torn scraps of newspaper, and so on. This variation also helps more fidgety and kinesthetic students to concentrate.

■ Try using the storyline technique for other forms of writing such as essays for science topics, argumentative essays, and so on.

Concept

Extending the line

The beginning – middle – end storyline is a basic template. You can increase the creative and intellectual challenge to your students by making it more sophisticated in various ways.

- 'Danger' as used in the diagram on p9 is a story ingredient. These ingredients are inclusions which alter the emotional tone of a narrative without being structural features (see p20 for more on this). Other common ingredients are humour, mystery, violence (see TIP), apprehension, secrecy, unease, and so on. These can be employed in an artfully vague way to suggest mood and atmosphere, leaving students to work on character, plot and setting.

- Place the B for Beginning some way along the storyline. This introduces the narrative refinement of flashback. What lies before the B can be a 'prequel', or a 'back story' which is referred to perhaps only fleetingly in the narrative.

- Parallel lines (drawn on a large sheet of paper!) create the opportunity to plot the same story from the viewpoints of different characters. Or, subsidiary lines linked to the main storyline allow students to plan subplots in a visual way.

The graphic on p19 shows these ideas. Solid vertical lines indicate features that we would expect students to include in any good story.

> ### TIP:
> One way of curbing the excessive use of violence in boys' writing is to give the writer some plastic money and suggest that he can have '£3 of violence' in his story. Be prepared to haggle over the cost of shootings, stabbings, and so on. The technique works very effectively in some cases.

Application

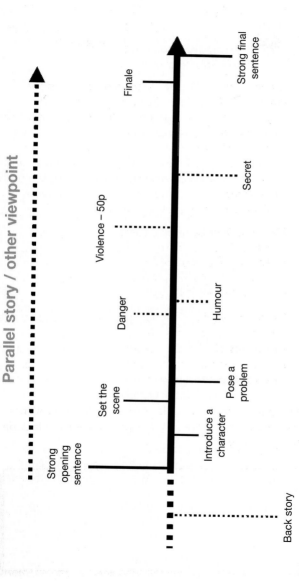

Parallel story / other viewpoint

Strong opening sentence

Set the scene

Introduce a character

Pose a problem

Danger

Humour

Violence – 50p

Secret

Finale

Strong final sentence

Back story

Concept

Story building – the basic elements of narrative

The folklorist Vladimir Propp (in *Morphology of the Folktale*) shows how comparative studies of traditional stories reveal a number of basic structural elements in narrative.

These are…

- Hero(ine) – the protagonist, a basic force of goodness and the noble qualities.

- Villain(ess) – the antagonist, a force for evil.

- Problem – the villain creates a problem that the hero must resolve.

- Journey – the hero embarks on a journey (often literal and symbolic) to resolve the problem.

- Partner – both hero and villain may have a partner. This creates the opportunity for dialogue and subplotting 'organically'.

- Help – this may be required by any character and may come in the form of other characters, accident and circumstance, or the supernatural (the gods intervening, for example).

- Knowledge / Power – the gaining and losing of the advantage among the characters keeps the narrative interesting.

- Object – this may be a physical object that must be found, destroyed, brought home, and so on. It is also the symbolic object of the hero's quest, to return home empowered and with the problem resolved.

Application

■ Ask students to think of one of their favourite stories to identify some or all of Propp's narrative elements.

■ Use genre grids (see p24) to link narrative elements to more specific plots within a genre.

■ Use yes-no coin flips to ask questions about narrative elements. Mind mapping the information organizes it effectively in a highly visual way.

■ Invite students to think of variations on the use of the basic elements. For example, the hero becomes evil, the villain's partner betrays the villain, the villain disguises himself as the hero, and so on.

■ Propp identifies a number of traditional 'sub elements' in his book. For example, 'A rule is broken', 'The hero is approached with a request or demand', 'A false hero appears', and so on.

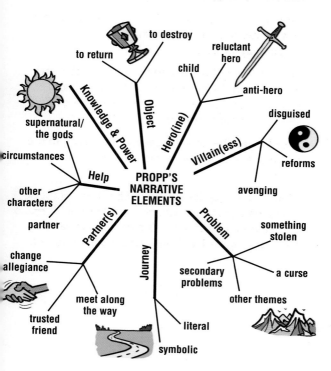

Concept

The six big important questions

The six big important questions are, of course, where, when, who, what, why and how. Encouraging students to question in this way creates a powerful tool for generating and organizing ideas at any stage of storymaking.

- Asking the six big important questions creates insights when writing needs to be done based on minimal information – for example, when students have to write a story, description, article, and so on from a given title or opening sentence.

- Use these questions in conjunction with a picture stimulus. So using p7 as an example: Why is the man with the sword attacking the other person? When is this story set? How might the victim get out of danger? What connections might there be between the man with the sword and the other man behind him?

- Encourage students to ask some of these questions in relation to the way they engage with writing. So, for example, 'Where and when do I produce my best writing?' 'Why is this?' 'What kind of planning works best for me?' 'Whose opinions about my work are of most use to me, and why?'

TIP:
Ask colleagues to encourage the same questioning attitude across the age, ability and subject range of the school.

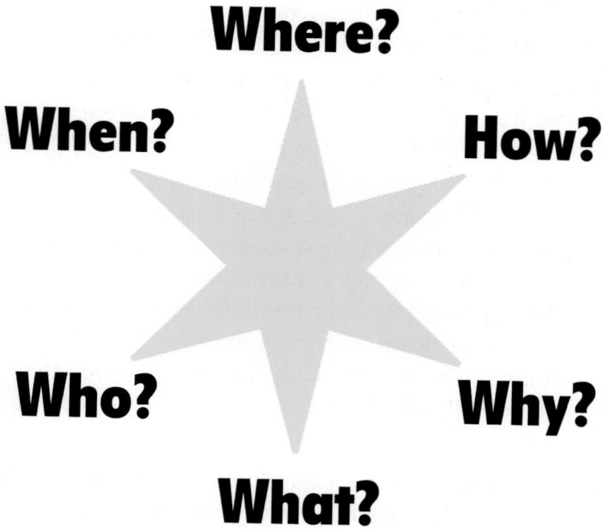

Where?

When?

How?

Who?

Why?

What?

Six big important questions

Concept

Exploring genre

Visual grids form an easy and effective way of helping students to explore Fantasy, Science Fiction and other genres. The visual nature of the resource means that students quickly become familiar with the 'motifs' of the genre (see below) and can immediately generate their *own* ideas rather than relying too much on material that already exists.

The Mystery Thriller grid on p25 is an example of a visual organizer, which is to say that lots of information is arranged so that all of it is available at a glance. Students can 'gather the gist' and form an overview, and make links between the boxes more or less simultaneously. Each box contains a motif. A motif is a constituent feature that helps to define and describe the larger domain, in this case a genre.

When creating genre grids, use a mixture of pictures and age-appropriate words. Include some motifs that are specific to the genre, some general words and pictures, and a few that are deliberately ambiguous – in the example given the words 'trip' and 'safe' serve that function. Students can of course construct their own grids for a favoured genre, or even use motifs taken from a story with which they are already familiar. You can develop the use of these grids by…

- Choosing motifs at random using dice. Roll a dice twice to find the co-ordinates of any box. You can use the grid to explore Propp's basic narrative elements by suggesting to students that whichever motif the dice chooses will reveal something about the hero / villain / problem, and so on.

- For a sequence of events, start in the top left-hand corner and move in a zigzag down the grid (like Snakes & Ladders backwards). Roll the dice once each time. The first motif selected will reveal something about how the story starts, the second motif will reveal something about what happens next, and so on.

Mystery Thriller grid

Concept

Creative overlaps

One useful definition of creative thinking is 'to go beyond the given'. The notion has many applications. Most of them encourage us to be unconventional in our ideas, this includes bringing new elements into conventional scenarios and using conventional elements in new ways.

I want to emphasize right away that being unconventional doesn't simply mean being different for its own sake. The haiku poet Matsuo Basho said that when we have learned the rules well, then we can bend them. I think this is an essential point to keep in mind. Unconventionality that arises from lack of understanding usually leads to limited outcomes, or to predictable outcomes that have a 'gloss' of being different. On the other hand truly going beyond the given – *based on an understanding of the given* – can lead to some startlingly original ideas.

> **TIP:**
> Benjamin Bloom's well-known taxonomy of thinking skills identifies *synthesis* as a high-order kind of thinking. The technique of creative overlaps explored here encourages students to create something new out of ideas they have previously understood and can increasingly master.

Application

■ Look again at the Mystery Thriller grid (p25). Use this as a template for students to create further grids from different genres. Then take two grids, say Romance and Science Fiction. Use dice rolls to choose a few items from each grid. We now have a mixture of Romance and SF motifs. What 'combo narratives' do they suggest?

■ Have students search for stories that combine genres. For example, the *Artemis Fowl* books written by Eoin Colfer are described as 'Techno Fantasy', a clever blend of Fantasy characters and modern technology. And the hugely popular *Alien* films combine SF scenarios with the Horror motif of being chased along dark corridors by terrifying monsters.

■ Go beyond the given by morphing known stories into different forms. How might the story of *Cinderella* be told as a series of text messages between Cinders and the Prince? Could the plot of *Romeo and Juliet* be turned into a series of local newspaper articles about the disruption caused in the town by the Capulets and Montagues (and would ASBOs be issued?).

Concept

Mental zoom tool

Some people develop the habit of thinking in 'big chunks'.
They might easily generate 'overview ideas' for whole
stories but have trouble thinking at the level of small detail.
A perfect example can be found in the opening shots of
the *Star Wars* movies, where a description of 'Long long
ago in a galaxy far away' drifts away into the starry
background. Back-cover blurbs also attempt to embrace
the entire tale in a few big chunk sentences.

Conversely, other students imagine and visualize in small
chunks. They like to work with details but might have
trouble conceptualizing the whole story. But these are just
habits of thought. Students can learn to think at various
levels of detail by practising mental zoom tool techniques.

Application

- Refer to p7. Pretend you can step into the picture. Now float up in the air and look down on the whole harbour scene. What else do you notice?

- Imagine there is a person in the building to the left, looking out at this scene. Use yes-no coin flips to find out five things about what this person looks like.

- Pretend that the man being attacked has a moneybag in his pocket. It contains five kinds of coins that you have never seen before. Imagine those coins and describe them.

- Leap ahead in the picture ten years. How have things changed?

- Pick a genre (using a genre grid perhaps) and write some 'overview' sentences, such as...

  - The crime boss moved into a new city and intended to gain control.

  - Time was running out for the factory owner to pay his protection money.

  - The poker game lasted all night and fortunes were won and lost.

- Now use the same grid and write about small details...

  - The golden goblet was decorated with six gems – two blue, two red and two white.

  - The man's handwriting – in blue fountain pen – was small and neat and sloped to the left.

  - The magnifying glass showed a smudged fingerprint on the edge of the stolen picture.

Concept

The filmic eye

We can all visualize even if some people are predominantly auditory or kinesthetic (as opposed to visual) thinkers. We can develop this ability in the following ways.

- Using a picture stimulus (let's look at p7 again), prepare a series of instructions to encourage students to visualize. For example…Turn left and walk away from the harbour. Continue for 20 paces. Notice something interesting to your right. Carry on for ten paces. You see a flight of stone steps to your left. Climb them. There are 13 steps. At the top is an old wooden door. Push it open. You step into a darkened room. A tallow lamp casts a dim amber light. There is a table in front of you. On the table is a parchment. You can read the words. The parchment says…

This act of imagination is what students do anyway as they listen to a story. Have students write their own short visualizations to share with classmates.

- Use the 'filmic eye' technique as illustrated on p31. Suggest to students that they are writers, directors and principal cameramen of a movie. Use a picture stimulus to focus attention. Have students use their imaginary cameras for a slow close-up of, say, the man being attacked. You notice more details of his face now – What are they? Do a slow 360° pan. What details move into view?

BCU	Big close-up
Cut	Change from one scene to another
Fade	Turning up or down sound / picture
Long shot	View showing the whole scene
Mix	Blend one picture into another
Pan	Moving panoramically up, down or sideways
POV	Point of view
Zoom	Drawing away or closer-in

The filmic eye

Descriptive writing

3

Concept

'Well in my opinion...'
– author intrusion

Author intrusion is the imposition of the writer's views directly into what should be 'neutral' text. Compare these two sentences...

- The western horizon blazed with the reds and yellows of a vivid sunset.

- The western horizon blazed with a beautiful display of reds and yellows.

In the first case 'vivid' is a more neutral term simply indicating the brilliance of the colours. In the second sentence the use of 'beautiful' conveys the author's opinion. This is author intrusion. All writing of course is an expression of what the author thinks and feels, so in that sense it will reflect the writer's 'voice' and world view. But writers still need to be aware of how their attitudes and opinions are woven into the work.

In non-fiction writing, analysing for bias and assumption is a valuable critical skill (for more detail see for instance *Teach Them Thinking* by Fogarty and Bellanca). Sometimes an author's views can subtly suggest or persuade while the thrust of the account or argument seems to be evenly balanced and objective. To know when a persuasive voice is speaking to us 'between the lines' can make a great difference to our own assessment of what is being said.

In fiction, the author's views can be expressed through characters, either directly in the first person, or using third person narrative overview to convey what characters think and feel.

All authors aim to explore and explain what sense they have made of their experience and of themselves. Descriptive writing is not just about conjuring up an image of what something looks and sounds like, but at best endeavours to capture and express something of its uniqueness.

Application

- Raise students' awareness of how opinions can be expressed artfully in fiction. So, for example…

  - America has always been a wild yet exciting place (author intrusion).

  - Ben felt that America had always been a wild yet exciting place (character's opinion expressed through third person narrative overview).

  - 'America has always been a wild yet exciting place,' Ben said (opinion expressed directly in the first person).

- Analyse scientific / supposedly neutral and objective text for opinion, bias, assumption, and so on. (An example I found immediately in an astronomy book on my shelf is 'Most of our trouble with the calendar can be blamed on the Moon.)

- Look at newspaper articles and journalistic writing in the same way. When are opinions and persuasions hiding in supposedly neutral reportage?

- Ask students to write descriptive pieces, then compose second versions full of their own opinions and feelings.

Concept

Metaphor and description

'The icy wind nipped at his face.' 'Nipped' of course is a metaphor. A direct comparison is being made between the pain caused by the cold wind and a similar pain that a small animal's teeth might inflict. Our language is riddled with metaphor, so much so that metaphors often go unrecognized as we read, speak and write.

There is a fine line between the elegant use of metaphor and author intrusion (or should that be a grey area?). What if I had said 'The icy wind attacked his face with tiny needles'? The imagined sensation of the wind feels the same to me in both sentences (although it may not to you). But there are also plenty of implied differences. In the first sentence 'nipped' might be a playful kittenish nip. In the second sentence 'attacked' is more violent, while the use of 'needles' suggests all kinds of – to me mainly unpleasant – associations.

The subject of metaphor in language is huge. As a start, it might be worth pointing out to students that –

- *All* language is representational. The word is not the thing itself.

- One carefully placed metaphor can save many words of straight description. (This is the minimal writing ploy in another guise!)

Application

Use the grid below to suggest how metaphor can be used in description. Describe a landscape as an animal, for example, or music as though it were a person – see also synaesthesia on p38.

	Person	Animal	Landscape	Weather	Music	Feeling
Person						
Animal						
Landscape						
Weather						
Music						
Feeling						

Metaphors and descriptive writing

Concept

Thumbnails and VAK

In computer terms a thumbnail is a small simple representation of something more elaborate and complex. In the context of writing a thumbnail is a short piece of description, dialogue, action, and so on (perhaps with an accompanying picture or visual motif) which acts as a prompt for more extended writing.

Creating thumbnails is a useful writing task in itself, of course. If you run the activity only three times a year with a class, then you'll have a bank of around 100 examples that can be used with other groups. If the thumbnails are printed on card and laminated, the resource becomes more attractive and durable.

When asking students to write thumbnails:...

- Encourage the use of multisensory language (visual, auditory and kinesthetic references).

- Remember that crisp metaphors can save lots of writing.

- Use story 'ingredients' (see p18) to hook the reader's curiosity.

> **TIP:**
> Many colour and black-and-white pictures can be found in the CD resource that accompanies *ALPS StoryMaker* and *StoryMaker Catch Pack*.

Application

Below is a standard 'descriptive thumbnail', plus the technique used for character and dialogue.

Mist and Steps

The mist wrapped around me like a cold damp cloak. Moonlight made drifting ghosts of the low cloud. The air was utterly still. Then came the sound of slow careful footsteps as someone *or something* approached…

Meeting at Midnight

"So, Baxter, you've arrived… Have you brought it?"

"I might have. Show me the money first, Connors."

"Don't get clever. You know the deal!"

"The terms have changed. You want the goods? You show me the cash."

"I see. Well, if that's how you intend to play the game…"

The Warrior

True name: Unknown.
Known as: Silent Blade
Background: Born into the Amazonoids clan. Veteran of the East Zone Dragon-Raptor wars. Currently Mercenary Warrior roaming the wastes of the Moebius Hills.
Strength: 8 *Cunning:* 10 *Powers:* 5
Weapons: 6 *Magic:* 0

Concept

'The colour of saying' – synaesthesia

If the word *kitiki* had a shape, what kind of shape would it be? If explorers discovered a new kind of creature in the Amazon rainforest and named it a baloobah, what would it look like?

If you thought that a *kitiki* looked something like this –

and a *baloobah* looked something like this –

then you share your impressions with most other people. You probably made sense of the words by (perhaps unconsciously) matching letter shapes and sequences with sounds, using hand gestures to 'mould out' the shapes in the air, plus using associations and comparisons. In other words you were demonstrating *synaesthesia*.

This is the tendency we have to understand the world in a multisensory way. We use 'all of ourselves' to make sense of things, and that includes cross-matching sensory impressions. If you asked your group 'What colour is anger?' it would not be a meaningless question. Most students would probably give you the same answer. Linking moods with colours is one example of synaesthesia. By the same token, what do these words have in common – undertones, sharp, earthy, big, backbone, flabby, austere? They are all terms used by wine connoisseurs to describe the smell and taste of wine – yet notice how they also relate to mood, shape, size and space, smell, texture, sound and anatomy.

As a tool for improving writing, the idea of synaesthesia is versatile and innovative. Why use only visual references to describe visual impressions? Why just describe sounds using sound-related words? Play with cross-matching the senses. Ask students to describe a feeling in terms of shape, or a sound in terms of a colour. Use the cross-match grid on p39 to create more original descriptions.

	Sight	Sound	Smell/Taste	Touch/Movement	Feeling
Feeling					
Touch/Movement					
Smell/Taste					
Sound					
Sight					

Cross-match grid

Concept

Atmosphere and mood

A piece of advice often given to emerging writers is *show don't tell*. I take that to mean 'give your readers an experience of the story (or whatever) rather than just talking about it'. It's easy to say 'The man felt uneasy as he walked along the deserted street', or 'It was a very spooky looking house'. The writer has told us these things, but it's left to us the readers to experience unease or the feeling of 'being spooked'.

This highlights the relationship between *author* and *authority*. Authors have to go into the worlds they want to write about and experience the mood and atmosphere for themselves through the use of memory and the power of imagination. What details of what you see, hear, feel, and so on, evoke feelings in you? These are the details you feed back into your writing to try and put your readers through the same experience.

Tools such as metaphor and synaesthesic language can help to create such experiences, but at the heart of the process is the writer's sensitivity to feelings, details that evoke them and 'reaching for the right words' to convey them.

Application

- Look back to the *Mist and Steps* thumbnail on p37. Pretend that the narrator is slightly uneasy. What are the physical aspects of his unease? What details of the scene draw out that uneasiness? Now pretend that the narrator is very frightened. Go through the same steps as above. What can we as writers say to make our readers feel our character's fright?

- Look ahead to p63. Notice the jug propped there by the barrel. It contains some red wine. Pretend I have never smelled or tasted red wine. What will you say to make me smell and taste it now?

- Describe eating a sweet of your choice so that my mouth will water and I really want to have one of those sweets.

- Describe the difference between the sound of a small two-stroke trial bike and a 1000cc motorbike.

- Ask students to create other examples like those above and to concentrate on using words to give their readers *experiences*.

Concept

Show don't tell

'Show don't tell' is given as standard advice to aspiring writers. To say 'The darkness made Smith feel very frightened' is simply to tell the reader that Smith was frightened. To show it implies re-creating for the reader Smith's *experience* of fear. In other words the aim of 'showing' is to make the reader go through it too.

This is sometimes easier said than done. To evoke (in this case) fear in the reader, we must call up that feeling within ourselves. Another piece of standard advice to writers is to 'write what you know'. If I have known fear in some form, then I can use that experience to guide the language that may re-create it in my readers. If I am writing a vampire story, I might never have encountered a vampire in reality, but I can make my story more powerful by evoking the victim's fear and horror, and the vampire's sense of hunger and loneliness (given that I have experienced those states in some way).

And that is the ongoing challenge for any writer – to generate feelings in himself and, through the artful use of words, to re-create them again and again in his readers.

Application

- Encourage students to visualize. Develop this as a mental skill. Take an example that most if not all students have experienced. Say, walking along the dunes overlooking a dramatic seascape. Have students remember their experience of that. Ask them to notice how they felt on those occasions. How would they describe those feelings to others? How would they create those feelings in someone who has never walked along dunes like that? What details of the imagined scene evoke the feelings in the students? – Those details can be fed back into the language they use to re-create the feelings in others.

- Use the technique of 'pretend this person has never...'. So imagine the smell of a rose. How would you describe that to someone who has never smelled a rose? Tip: Look at p38 on synaesthesia for some insights.

- Encourage the use of simile, metaphor and analogy to describe feelings and states. Search for examples of these, such as how features of the landscape and weather are used to describe people's moods and feelings.

Concept

Viewpoints

Writing from different viewpoints keeps thinking flexible and exercises the imagination. We've already looked at first person and third person writing within the context of author intrusion (p32). These techniques rely upon different viewpoints for their effect. The 'choose your own adventure' game (p66) makes good use of second person writing (the you-voice).

These are conventions of form. The idea of viewpoints goes further than this and involves more radical leaps of the imagination.

Application

- Look at the picture below. Suggest to students that as they float into the picture they are burglars. What thoughts and feelings do they experience? Float back out. Now float in again and pretend to be elderly people living alone. What thoughts and feelings do you have?

- Imagine you could stand on that street corner and accelerate time. A year goes by in ten seconds. What do you notice?

- Be a leaf dropping from a tree. Describe your experience.

- Imagine gravity was cut by 66 per cent so that things happen in slow motion. Drop a bottle of water. Describe what you see and hear.

- Imagine you are the old stone wall in the picture. Write a short diary account of what you have witnessed.

Creating convincing characters 4

Concept

Some top tips

Characters that appear in students' work are sometimes nothing more than names (this is the worst-case scenario) with perhaps a few details of external appearance added. The next level of sophistication makes use of stereotypes. These may include personality traits, feelings and thoughts, but are derivative and used 'off the peg' without much reflection or modification to the basic template.

As the writer Alan Garner has said, 'People are like onions – they have layers'. Once young writers appreciate this and begin to apply it in their work, their characters will become more diverse, more believable and more true-to-life.

This section of the book explores ways of enriching characters. It's worth mentioning at the outset that not everything a student learns about his characters needs to be put into his stories or plays. What's important is that the writer is *informed* about them – that is, knows more than appears (or needs to appear) in the work. Carefully selected character details sprinkled artfully through the writing will make the most impact.

How to become more informed? Be nosy…

When we look at any person we see the surface of a rich and complex inner world of thoughts, feelings and experiences. Simply to have that insight leads to a greater respect for others. To respect here is to 'look again', to see and appreciate more. This willingness to look again is of importance in any writer's attitude.

Application

■ Flip through a telephone directory and choose a surname and first name at random; imagine what that person would look like.

■ Notice people. Scribble down little details like the colour of someone's eyes, the shape of their mouth when they smile, the smell of their perfume or cologne.

■ Time hop. Imagine what an older person would have looked like when (s)he was younger, and vice versa.

■ Listen to snippets of conversation and imagine how that conversation might continue. Notice how people speak – is the voice high or low pitched, are the words spoken quickly or slowly, are there lots of 'ahs' and 'ums' in between, the so-called 'conversational fillers'?

■ Take one detail from ten different people and put them all together in a description of an imaginary character. If the character doesn't work, decide what you need to change.

■ When you go shopping for clothes, look at some items that you would never wear: imagine the person who would wear them.

■ Read the work of other authors and notice how they create believable characters. Write your observations down for future reference.

■ Play a piece of instrumental music that you don't know. Ask yourself 'If this music were a person, what would that person be like?'

■ Imagine a 'what if' situation involving a character you are developing. For instance, finding a wallet with a hundred pounds just lying there in the street. What do you think your character would do, and why? What if there were no clues about the owner in the wallet? What if your character realized the wallet belonged to someone (s)he disliked? Think of other 'what if' variations to really get into the mind and motivations of your character.

Concept

Character cards

Characters develop over time. By the end of a good novel we feel we know the people we met there. This is character development at a professional level. There's no reason why our students can't aspire to create characters that are more than just tokens or icons: young writers too can learn about their characters as the work evolves.

Here are some ideas to boost that process.

- We separate characters, settings and plot to make planning easier and clearer, but it's an artificial distinction. We can actually learn about any aspect of the story by looking at any other aspect. Thinking about plot will give insights into characters' motivations. Thinking of setting yields ideas about what the characters there might be thinking and feeling.

- Introduce the idea of character types. These are not stereotypes (although they may begin that way), but characters that appear in a number of stories. They grow and change over time because of their experiences, and as the writer herself grows and changes. This means that the writer will get to know these characters in more and more detail. It is sometimes the case that character types represent aspects of the writer's own personality, or how the writer was at some past stage of her life. See the page opposite for examples.

- Character cards. These might be very simple (see Thumbnails on p37) and the characters mere icons, or they can be more layered descriptions which the author adds to as the story develops.

Application

4

Character types

Character types are thematic or generic characters that might appear in various guises throughout a range of stories. They differ from stereotypes in being used deliberately and mindfully.

Tony

- ◆ Tony is usually between 11 and 14.

- ◆ He is quite tall, dark haired and dresses 'quietly'.

- ◆ He keeps himself to himself. He has a few close friends but doesn't mix easily.

- ◆ He loves to learn and is an expert in some areas, usually science and the supernatural.

Eleanor

- ◆ Eleanor is usually a couple of years older than Tony.

- ◆ She is tall, fair and pretty but doesn't think she is.

- ◆ She is open and friendly, but has some deep secrets and fears.

- ◆ When she is tested to the limit, she finds strengths that even she didn't know about.

Concept

Dear diary

Exploring characters can be enriched by varying the form that writing about them takes. A diversity of writing tasks also tends to sustain a writer's interest for longer. Here are some suggestions...

- Write some diary entries in role as a character you are planning to put into a story (or a character, from a book or a film, for example, that you know well). Write a diary in role as one character gossiping about another character.

- Write a series of letters, texts or emails between two or more of your characters.

- Make a shopping list itemizing things that a character of yours wants to buy.

- Some people leave post-it notes about the house as reminders. What would be written on your character's post-its?

- Write a short newspaper article featuring one or more of your characters (see p82 for more tips on doing this).

- On the opposite page are some of the things a character keeps in his / her pockets. What can you work out about that person based on these? (This is a useful thinking-skills activity too, insofar as students will be deducing, inferring, speculating, and so on.)

Application

What do these items tell you about a character?

➤ A donor card.

➤

➤ A coin cut carefully in half.

➤

➤ A repeat prescription for strong painkillers.

➤

➤ A first class return rail ticket to London.

➤

Concept

People are like onions – exploring character in more depth

The template on the opposite page is more than just a writing frame. It acts as a visual metaphor suggesting that people, like onions, have layers. Furthermore, implicit in the design is the idea that our personality supports our appearance, our background supports (that is, influences) our personality, and so on.

When I introduce the template I make it clear that the students must write only inside the sections of the pyramid. This is another example of the 'minimal writing' strategy. Here are some more tips for using the technique.

- Basic identifiers means a couple of brief descriptive details. If the character walked into the room, what two things would you notice about him / her first?

- The 'one special detail' box is filled in last, when the students know more about the character. What's special might be thoughts, feelings or some future achievement, for example.

- Coin flips can introduce unanticipated ideas into the exploration. Heads = yes, tails = no. Ask ten closed questions about any aspect of your character and record the information in the appropriate sections.

- Exploring background creates an opportunity to develop timelines. Exploring future possibilities creates an opportunity to develop decision trees.

TIP:
If you run this activity just three times in a year you'll have a bank of around 100 detailed character profiles to use with other groups.

Application

1 Basic identifiers.

2 One special detail.

3 Physical description.

4 Personality (thoughts, feelings, traits, beliefs, and so on).

5 Background.

6 Future possibilities.

7 Core values and motivations.

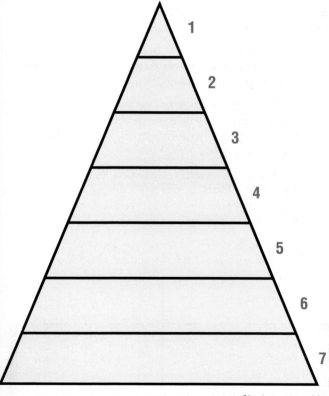

Character pyramid

Concept

Character collage

Refer to the page opposite. Ask students to notice what's contained within the rectangle, then suggest that these are thoughts going on inside a person's mind. Why is (s)he thinking these thoughts, and why is (s)he thinking about these things in this way?

This activity also invites speculation, interpretation, inferring, and so on. Explain to the students that there are no right answers to this exercise, it's simply about trying to work out what's on this character's mind.

TIP:

Students can easily make character collages of their own by pasting images from comics, newspapers and magazines onto sheets of paper. Or they can be created on the computer by importing clipart into a Word document. 3D versions using pieces of materials and small objects bring a more 'kinesthetic' dimension to the activity.

Application

Concept

'Bundles of contradictions'

When the writer Aldous Huxley was asked for his definition of a human being he said we are all 'bundles of contradictions' – unlike onions! He also said that the only truly consistent people are dead. Using the technique below allows students to create rich and diverse characters very easily…

- Make a list of characteristics – you don't have to use the ones in my example (see opposite). For each characteristic roll a dice and use the number to make a mark on the line. Very soon you will have created a fascinating character profile for further discussion. Note: make it clear to students that the numbers 1–6 aren't precise units of measurement, but rather more vague units of comparison and proportion.

- The technique creates the opportunity to explore the meanings of words. What meanings might 'strong' have for instance? What could be the differences between 'clever' and 'intelligent'?

- Having created the character, deliberately alter one or two characteristics. What other characteristics might change as a consequence? By how much? Why?

- Draw out two character profiles at random and write an imaginary dialogue between them.

Application

How...

	1	2	3	4	5	6
Tall	←————————————————→
Strong	←————————————————→
Smart	←————————————————→
Wealthy	←————————————————→
Powerful	←————————————————→
Attractive	←————————————————→
Popular	←————————————————→
Confident	←————————————————→
Intelligent	←————————————————→
Selfish	←————————————————→
Cunning	←————————————————→
Evil	←————————————————→

is your character?

Writing games

Concept

The ten sentence game

Activities where there is flexibility within a structure allow creative writing to develop more quickly. Tasks that are too prescriptive (such as filling in words missing from a sentence) limit thinking. Exercises that remain too vague (such as making up a story from a title) can leave students floundering. Young writers need to have sure and robust guidance for their thinking, but with enough 'space' for them to have their own ideas.

The ten sentence game is one such example. The sentences are 'artfully vague' – we are given precise pieces of information but each sentence also begs many questions.

- A shot rang out.
- He called her name.
- It was lost.
- And that was only the beginning.
- The door opened without a sound.
- It couldn't be true.
- Glass shattered nearby.
- There was a gasp of amazement.
- It missed by inches.
- They shook hands on the deal.

'What level must you reach to be an author?' 'The level of happiness.' Developing as a writer is about playing with ideas, and being nosy about the effects that language has on one's thoughts, feelings and perceptions. But at the heart of creative writing lies fun and the love of a good challenge.

Application

- The most basic use of the list is to ask students to build a story using the ten sentences in the given order. But the list is more versatile than that...

- Plan a story using the sentences in reverse order.

- Specify the kind of story to be planned – Science Fiction or Fantasy, for example.

- Supply some of the sentences and leave other bullet points blank. Students supply ideas for the missing sentences (and then plan a story using all sentences).

- Use a sequence of pictures instead of written sentences, or a combination of words and pictures.

- Take one or more sentences and apply the 'six big important questions' (see p22). Use coin flips and closed questioning (heads = yes, tails = no) to generate more information.

- Use the sentences with the storyline technique (see p16 and p18). Arrange the sentences along the entire line, or concentrate them into one small section of the narrative.

- Use the sentences with genre grids (see p24), selecting motifs through decision or chance to add detail to each sentence.

- Combine the sentences with motifs from familiar stories (popular books and films, for instance) to capitalize on students' often extensive knowledge of these.

- Encourage students to create their own ten-sentence lists for use with other groups.

Concept

Comic book dialogue

Use comics and graphic novels. Remove the words from the speech and thought bubbles. Students then pick up context clues from the pictures to suggest dialogue.

Application

■ **Comic cut-ups** Cut up the pages of comic books into separate panels. Students must arrange the panels into an order that makes narrative sense (this may not be the order in which the panels were arranged originally!).

■ **Dialogue visualization** Students are asked to imagine the setting, characters' appearance, and so on, based on a sequence of dialogue.

■ **Font work** Using computers, ask students to consider various font styles and the 'mood' of dialogue they might best be suited to. So for example…

  – Comic Sans MS is rounded, buoyant and jolly.

  – CHASM IS RAGGED, EDGY AND MORE SINISTER.

  – *BALLOONIST IS TALL, BOLD AND ASSERTIVE.*

  – *Amaze is flowing, elegant and dignified.*

■ **Speech bubbles** Show students different examples of speech and thought bubbles – as shown on the opposite page – and ask how the shape and style of the bubbles matches the mood of the words they contain.

Concept

Collecting motifs

Motifs are constituent features that help to define and describe a genre. They may be, for example, snippets of dialogue, descriptions of place, objects, character details. Motifs can act as a kind of shorthand to quickly establish a setting or situation without the need to create it from scratch in laborious detail. So, for example…

- The tumbleweed rolled down the dusty deserted street. A lone horseman dressed all in black rode slowly, silently into town.

- Lightning flickered about the ramparts of the mountaintop castle. A wolf howled mournfully from the depths of the endless forest.

- The main engines engaged with a roar. Through the viewport the star patterns wheeled around. 'Reverse the polarity of the neutron flow!' the captain yelled desperately.

- Jeff Creed tilted his homburg so that its shadow fell across his eyes. He flicked up the collar of his raincoat, then lit a cigarette and watched its smoke rise lazily into the still night-time air.

The downside of using motifs in this way is that they can lead to cliché and stereotyping (as my examples clearly demonstrate!). But more positively their use allows students to become familiar with the conventions of different genre and lessens the time and effort needed to move a story along.

TIP:
The resource CDs accompanying *ALPS StoryMaker* and *StoryMaker Catch Pack* feature a number of genre grids and black-and-white pictures.

Application

- Video clips. Collect (or have students collect) scenes from films or TV series that illustrate the use of motifs.

- Build a bank of motifs from comic books, graphic novels, and so on. How are they used to establish time, place, mood, character?

- Use collections of motifs in genre grids (see p24) to create a range of narratives.

- List motifs used in pictures, then offer the lists to other groups and ask them to imagine what picture they are suggesting. So for instance, in the picture below we have –

  - The lonely street
  - The rats in the alley
  - The bag being clutched
  - The scribbled note
  - The hurrying figure
  - The discarded bottle
  - Mysterious pursuit

Concept

Book titles and blurb it

Authors and publishers tend to think very carefully about titles and blurbs. The words and pictures making up the covers of a book form the 'first contact' that a reader has with the story, and must make an immediate positive impact.

Destination	Somewhere	Time
Alive	Legend	Nightmare
Fall	House	Journey
Centre	Lord	Fantastic
Creature	Call	Shadow
Road	Trade	Trick

Application

■ Analyse book blurbs for linguistic features and conventions (for example the overuse of superlatives – 'bestselling', 'international', 'unputdownable'). Compare blurbs from books of the same genre. Look at the blurbs of non-fiction books. What differences in style do you observe?

■ Encourage students to create blurbs for their own stories. Use blurbs from published work as springboards for students' own work.

■ Discuss the concept of blurbs. Why are they called 'blurbs'? Do blurbs make exaggerated claims? Create a catchy blurb made from sentences and phrases taken from a range of books.

■ Look at book and story titles. Study the visual style of the words. How can this enhance the impact of a title? Combine this research with font work (see p61).

■ Play with combinations to make up new titles that may spark ideas for stories – see the grid of suggestions below.

Man	Country	Machine
Darkness	Heart	Three
City	Encounter	Day
Forbidden	Beyond	Silent
Fall	Running	Storm
Another	Stars	Wild

Making titles

Concept

Choose your own adventure

Choose your own adventures (CYOAs) in the form of Fighting Fantasy Gamebooks, mostly written by Steve Jackson and Ian Livingstone, became extremely popular in the early 1980s and have remained so ever since. The narratives consist of numbered story fragments, sometimes only a few sentences in length, wherein the reader is faced with a dilemma and must make a decision. The reader's choice takes him to another fragment elsewhere in the book, where he faces the consequences of his actions.

The reader is also a player-character in the story. He can arm himself with various weapons, potions, amulets, and so on, which can be traded with other characters. But he can also lose these items and even his life if the wrong decisions are made.

Stories in this format are very engaging. I've known otherwise 'reluctant readers' to bury themselves in CYOA books for hours on end as they search for the route that lets them survive to the end of the tale. The same format can of course be exploited to motivate students to write. It would be wise to review a published fighting fantasy adventure before launching the activity. Obviously the students' stories will be much simpler than any Jackson / Livingstone title, but more elaborate stories can be built from very simple beginnings.

> **TIP:**
> See *The Warlock of Firetop Mountain* by Steve Jackson and Ian Livingstone on p96.

Application

To start a CYOA –

■ Use a visual organizer (as shown below). Each number corresponds to a paragraph that a student will write. The paragraph will feature a dilemma that requires a decision to be made. The decision will take the student to one of two other numbers. So for example – *You hear a sound farther along the dark corridor ahead. Do you investigate? (go to number 8) or do you avoid possible danger? (go to number 9)*. The plot is built up in this way.

■ Before starting, have students decide on a genre and a basic scenario.

■ Discuss possible problems, dangers, crises and dilemmas that might be encountered.

■ Plan ahead! Start at number 1. What happens? What decision needs to be made? Which other two numbers do the alternative choices lead to? Continue this step-by-step process until all the numbers are used up.

■ Make sure that one narrative route (combination of numbers) allows the reader-character to survive.

■ Write in the second person 'you-voice'.

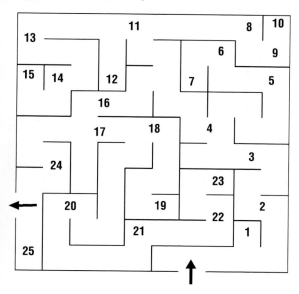

Concept

The mystery technique

A 'mystery' in this sense consists of scraps of information that students review and arrange to tell a story and / or solve a problem. In the example given on the opposite page, 'Who Stole the Kay-to-Bah Diamond?', 36 pieces of information map out the narrative and offer clues about which character, among a number of possibilities, may have committed the crime. Whodunnit mysteries like this are perhaps the easiest to construct.

If you want students to explore the technique in their writing, let them work through the Kay-to-Bah mystery first.

- Transcribe the 36 items, print off enough copies for your requirements and cut them up into separate pieces.

- Explain to students that they must decide which character most probably stole the diamond. To be a suspect a character must have had the means (how it was done), the opportunity (when it was done) and the motive (why it was done) – MOM.

- There is no single right answer to the puzzle.

Encourage students to arrange the information scraps into concept maps, gathering scraps by character or MOM. Alternatively in this case some pieces of information can be arranged along a timeline.

> **TIP:**
> For more information on concept and mind mapping see *Thinking for Learning* by Mel Rockett and Simon Percival, and to learn more about the mystery technique in a 'non-fiction' context, see *Theory into Practice: mysteries make you think* by David Leat and Adam Nicols.

Application

On Thursday October 14th at 6.42 p.m. the alarm went off at Kenniston City Museum.

The Museum closed at 5.00 p.m. The cleaning staff began their shift.

Alistair Harvey usually stays late at the Museum to finish his paperwork in peace.

By 6.55 p.m. on October 14th a police patrol car had arrived at the scene.

The Kay-to-Bah Diamond weighs 300 carats. It is currently valued for insurance purposes at £10 million.

Sergeant Mulholland and Officer Michalik discovered the theft of the Kay-To-Bah Diamond at 7.12 p.m.

Mulholland and Michalik offered to take the Museum's CCTV video tapes over to police Headquarters for safe keeping and later analysis.

In their latest funding review Kenniston City Council decided to cut grants to the Museum by 22%.

At 8.37 p.m. on October 14th Mulholland and Michalik's patrol car was involved in a RTA. Both officers were knocked unconscious but were otherwise unhurt.

A dark coloured saloon (blue or black according to one witness) was spotted driving away from the scene of the crash.

The Kay-To-Bah Diamond was once the centrepiece of the Double Crown of the Pharaoh Kharis the Third who ruled during the Twenty-Seventh Dynasty in Egypt.

Lisa Chamberlain was once Head of Development at Style Synthetics, one of Magnus Carmody's companies.

Lisa Chamberlain and Magnus Carmody were childhood sweethearts.

Magnus Carmody never forgave Albert Watts for taking Lisa away from him.

Ben Leech drives a dark green Ford saloon.

Magnus Carmody owns eight cars of various kinds.

Eleanor Harris told Ray Kane that Albert Watts and Magnus Carmody were always fierce rivals at school.

Alistair Harvey is due to retire at the end of the year.

Lisa Chamberlain left her job at Style Synthetics after marrying Albert Watts.

The evening cleaning team arrived at the museum between 5.00 and 5.15 p.m.

Ben Leech has student debts of £11,000 from his undergraduate years. He has taken a number of part-time jobs to help repay his loans.

Margus Carmody is currently being investigated by the Inland Revenue for a number of tax-related matters.

Magnus Carmody offered the Kay-To-Bah Diamond to the City Museum on permanent loan.

Unconfirmed reports allege that a diamond identical to the famous Kay-To-Bah Diamond was offered to a private collector in Japan early in October.

Lisa Watts never forgave Magnus Carmody for forcing her to leave her job at Style Synthetics after she married Albert Watts.

Vicki Stand discovered that Magnus Carmody went on a two week business trip to the Far East late in September.

Style Synthetics manufactures many items made from metal, glass and plastic.

Two years ago Ben Leech applied for a job at Style Synthetics and was interviewed by Magnus Carmody himself.

Three months ago £5000 was deposited into Leonard Beech's bank account.

Magnus Carmody has offered a £25,000 reward for the safe return of the Kay-To-Bah diamond. The jewel must be returned to him personally.

The Watts's own a dark blue Vauxhall Corsa hatchback.

Ben Leech has an uncle who is a jeweller.

Leonard Beech's father's brother has a jewellery shop and workshop in the nearby city of Clayton.

Concept

Riddles and nonsense words

Many books on accelerated ('brain based') learning make the point that students learn more effectively when they feel comfortable in the presence of ambiguity and uncertainty. Feeling the need to 'know the right answer right now' is a limiting behaviour that generates anxiety and creates deference to authority that is vested in simply knowing more. Scientific enquiry is all about exploring possibilities from a platform of partial understanding. Philosophical enquiry is even less inclined to predispose right or final answers.

Similarly in developing a robust and varied vocabulary and endeavouring to master the many interrelated skills of powerful communication, the preparedness to explore, experiment and play is more important than the urge to 'get it right' at the outset.

Pioneers such as Howard Gardner (see for instance *Multiple Intelligences: The Theory in Practice*) have raised awareness that the brain is flexible, versatile and 'wired up' to understand the world in various ways, including through words. We become linguistically intelligent by playing with language and noticing its effect upon others and ourselves.

So-called nonsense words offer a fine opportunity to play. When we see a made-up word like *glombous* for instance, how do we begin to make sense of it?

- By listening to its sounds.
- By looking at letter patterns and combinations.
- By association and memory.
- By mixing sensory impressions (that is, synaesthesically, see p38).

This is how language develops anyway.

Riddles too convey that tantalizing sense of hidden meaning and offer a doorway into the exploration of metaphor, symbol and pun. Both nonsense words and riddles can be used to clarify and strengthen students' creative attitude through language.

Application

■ Invite students to suggest meanings for words such as...

- *snoodled*
- *churdling*
- *squeshy*
- *opticus*
- *garrt*
- *voomacious*
- *bant.*

■ Read poems such as *Jabberwocky* by Lewis Carroll and the work of Charles Causeley. Encourage students to make up nonsense words of their own. This will test and develop their emergent understanding of grammar and syntax.

■ Play with riddles to develop confidence in exploring meaning. Here are a few of my favourites...

- Thirty-two white horses on the red hills. Now they stamp, now they champ, now they stand still (Answer: your teeth).

- Brothers and sisters have I none, but that man's father is my father's son (Answer: a boy looking in a mirror – that is, oneself).

- Charles the First walked and talked half an hour after his head was cut off. (The solution is in careful punctuation... Charles the First walked and talked. Half an hour after, his head was cut off. The next riddle is similar – but I'll leave you to work it out.)

- Every lady in the land has twenty nails upon each hand. Five and twenty upon hands and feet. All this is true without deceit.

Other forms and styles

Concept

Voice and style

In the same way that our spoken voices differ in many ways so too do our individual written 'voices' develop and strengthen over time. My own opinion is that a writer's voice is a more fundamental aspect of his work than his style. If I'm writing a story followed by a chapter of an educational book, my style in each case will obviously change a lot. My style will also vary between genres and will be influenced by pace, atmosphere, the necessity for dialogue, and so on. But whatever I write, I would hope that something distinct would be constantly present – an 'essence' that marks it out as a piece of Steve Bowkett's work.

Evolving a distinctive voice is a matter of time, patience, hard work and reflectiveness. These are the building blocks of experience. Even if most of your students have no long-term ambitions to write, it's worth encouraging and maintaining a clear intent to develop an individual voice, as this endeavour feeds back constantly into two vital factors in writing anything more effectively –

1. Regularity of practice.

2. Reaching for the right words during the flow of composition.

Application

The acronym VOICE will help to keep students focused –

V – variety. Read many authors and notice how they achieve their effects (that is, what happens to you mentally and emotionally as you read).

O – observation. Always read for pleasure, but sometimes look more critically at 'how the experts do it'. The nosier you are the more tips and trade secrets you'll pick up.

I – imitate. Copying the style of an author you admire helps you to create a voice of your own. Most accomplished writers copied their literary heroes as their own powers developed.

C – chill. Despite the pressures of syllabuses and exams, your writing skills cannot be forced. Be prepared to learn fast, but never struggle or strain – and never feel you've failed if things don't seem to be working out. Everything you do is another step along the road to success.

E – explore and experiment. Try new things and face writing challenges as an adventurer.

Concept

Be somebody else

Using pseudonyms is a great way of exploring what you can do with your writing. An ancient proverb says 'A man has as many faces as he has friends'. By the same token, you might consider that a writer has as many styles as he has pseudonyms.

I have personal experience of this. A number of years ago I was asked to write some adult horror fiction, with the expectation that it would contain quite explicit sexual content and plenty of gory violence. I accepted the challenge but found that I couldn't bring myself to do it… What if my family and friends found it? What if my pupils at school read the stuff! It was only when I decided to 'hide' behind a pseudonymous mask that I could relax and focus enough to produce the work.

In case you're wondering, my horror pseudonym was Ben Leech (a good tough name if I say so myself). I've used two other pseudonyms besides: Philippa Stephens for a teenage romance novel and Len Beech for a collaborative novel that I personally wasn't happy with.

Suggest the idea of pseudonyms to your students to help them assume the 'persona' of a writer of a certain genre or style.

Application

■ Notice how authors' (often real) names are used in marketing and promotion. For example, the pattern of two or three initials followed by a surname – J.R.R. Tolkien, C.S. Lewis, J.K. Rowling, G.P. Taylor.

■ Explore how an author's name creates an impression of the person. Notice too how real names or pseudonyms often 'fit' the kind of work that author produces – J.T. Edson, Zane Grey (Westerns), Storm Constantine (Fantasy), Isaac Asimov (Science Fiction).

■ Discuss why writers might use pseudonyms – for example, to experiment with different kinds of work. Stephen King wrote a clutch of more experimental novels under the name of Richard Bachman. Ruth Rendell explored more psychologically based crime fiction writing as Barbara Vine.

■ Decide what kind of writing you want to do and make up an appropriate pseudonym by looking in telephone directories, at books in the library, and so on. Once you've chosen a name, reflect on what part of your personality it best represents. How does it feel to write as that person?

■ If you really want to get into a pseudonym, look back to p46 and p50 to learn more about yourself. You might also find that your pseudonymous self makes a great character in some of your work.

Concept

The language of the subject

The notion of 'the language of the subject' is an extension of the ideas we've just been exploring. The language of, say, a scientific report is as much a 'genre' as a story of high fantasy, having its own style, conventions and protocols. Noticing, exploring and practising these allows young writers to tackle a greater range of writing tasks with more confidence.

Another salient point to be made here is that, as the educationalists Neil Postman and Charles Weingartner assert in *Teaching as a Subversive Activity*, any subject *is* its language. We express our understanding of, say, biology by using its vocabulary within the conventions of the subject's 'genre' – which are themselves part of the larger territory of 'scientific language'.

Encouraging students to express themselves in the language of any subject is a matter not only of developing the pertinent writing skills, but also of helping them to be *unafraid of ideas*. This is the key first step in the process. Beyond that, awareness of and practice in a range of thinking skills establishes the necessary mental toolkit for the job – try for instance my own *100 Ideas for Teaching Creativity* and *100 Ideas for Teaching Thinking Skills* as a first step.

Application

Take a rather bland and general sentence such as –

It rained all day.

How might a Horror writer embellish it?

What changes might a poet make to it?

What else could a geographer say to increase our understanding of what the sentence means?

Concept

Root maps

Exploring etymology quickly and powerfully generates insights into words and the organic and fluid nature of language. The whole notion of language trees and word webs reflects the fact that language isn't static, and that very largely what we regard as the conventions of correct or standard English, for example, boil down to the opinions of a number of (mainly long dead) academics. Bill Bryson in *Mother Tongue* speaks very passionately and eloquently on this topic. Insistence on technical 'correctness' simply generates stiltedness and pedantry, I feel, and at worse intensifies the 'fear of the wrong answer' that already inhibits learning in so many children.

We all own language. It is my sandpit too and I can play in it as much as I like. However, knowing where words come from and how they've evolved gives my play even greater learning value.

Application

■ Break words into bits to encourage sudden new insights. If we read 'information' as 'in-formation' for instance we can appreciate that knowledge works best when it's being formed into greater meanings and understandings.

■ Collect prefixes, suffixes and roots. Create a 6x6 grid and help students to make up new words. So, for example, what might these made-up words mean; *aquarette*, *scribatory*, *interport*, (to) *octofy*?

■ Create compound words for fantasy stories. Make one list of nouns and another of adjectives / verbs and play with combinations. So, for example, a little thought gives us Nightwatcher, Firetreader, Lightspinner, Moonwhisperer.

■ Explore nonsense words (see p70) and encourage students to make links with terms they already know. So with a word like *glombous*, the 'gl' sound reminds us of glue, glutinous, globe, globule, while the 'ous' pattern forms a description (often being 'full of') – adventurous, perilous, joyous, and so on.

■ Explain the evolution of certain words to students. Any good etymological dictionary will help with this – or refer again to the excellent *Mother Tongue* by Bill Bryson

■ Explore words that have many meanings, such as fast, set, sound, race, fine.

■ Foster a creative attitude to language within contexts that may already be familiar to students – slang terms from popular TV shows like *The Simpsons*, computer and electronic game terminology, telephone texting (txtng?) and fantasy wargaming.

Concept

Thinking poetry

Poetical thinking is not primarily about rhyme, metre, versification, and so on, but about the endeavour to capture the uniqueness of a person, place, object, moment... A vital part of such uniqueness is the emotional impact such a person or moment makes on the writer. True poetical thinking captures an essence, but it is of course possible simply to copy the conventions of form by imitating, for example, the verse structure of one of Thomas Hardy's poems or making up new nonsense words to fit into *Jabberwocky*.

There are many excellent books on writing poetry. A few I'd recommend are –

- *Teaching Poetry* by Fred Sedgewick, Classmates series, Continuum 2003
- Sandy Brownjohn's books:
  - *Does It Have To Rhyme?*, Hodder & Stoughton 1986
  - *The Ability To Name Cats*, Hodder & Stoughton 1993
  - *Word Games* (with Janet Whitaker), Hodder & Stoughton 1998.

Application

- Use the grid on p25 as a way of creating a poem around a chosen theme, which might also form the poem's title. The activity works best if the theme of the poem is a feeling or abstract idea. As an example we'll make a four-line poem called 'The Answer'.

- Each line will begin in the same way, with the words 'The answer is...'

- Roll a dice twice to select co-ordinates for a motif from the grid, starting at the bottom left. The picture selected should give you an idea for finishing the first line of the poem.

- Repeat the technique to complete the other three lines. Look back and tidy up.

This is the poem I made: your lines of course will be different.

4/4 The answer is a circle that will spin for ever more,

5/6 The answer is a long straight street lined with many doors.

5/4 The answer is a traveller who learns along the way.

1/6 The answer is a chequered game – who'll win it? Who can say?

Concept

Newspaper articles

Opposite is a simple template for helping students understand the structure of a newspaper article. Copy the template on to an A4 or A3 sheet and explain to the students that whatever they are reporting on, they can write only within the sections in the triangle.

- Headline. There is just room in the top section for a few high-impact words to grab the reader's attention. Dog Bites Man! The headline does not need to be a complete grammatically accurate sentence.

- Byline. One or two brief sentences which convey the sense of what the whole story is about.

- Key idea(s). A short paragraph for each main segment or key point of the story, arranged in a logical sequence.

- Development. Further details and an elaboration of the key points.

- Supplementary material. Editorial comment, quotes, subjective opinion, and so on.

Application

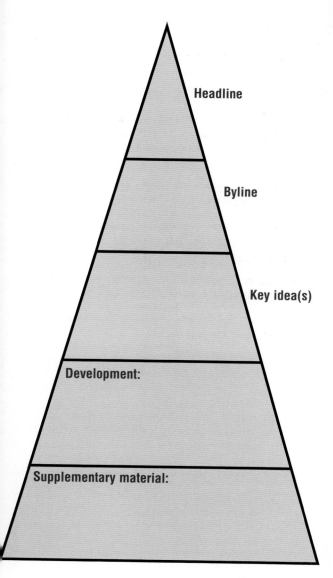

Newspaper articles

Concept

Thinking time, writing time, reviewing time

These three phases – thinking, doing, reviewing – are common to all creative processes.

The thinking at the start is not simply idle daydreaming, but 'systematic daydreaming'. The student has previously decided what to think about and now, in this quietly reflective state, notices the trains of thought drifting through his conscious awareness.

The mind-state for writing balances the ongoing stream of creative thoughts with the critical ability to select and organize the appropriate words during the flow of composition. That phrase is deliberate, since if the writing is a struggle then I feel that not enough prior thinking has been done.

After writing, the student needs to review the work as a piece of text. By and large the creative tap is turned off and evaluative critical thinking skills are applied.

These three stages are overlaid by the two broader phases of 'harvesting' ideas and then organizing them to the point where the project is finished.

> **TIP:**
> Although the notion of redrafting is popular in the teaching of creative writing, if the thinking time is spent effectively and if students 'go with the flow' of composition and review honestly, multiple redrafts are rarely required. Some authors write several drafts, but this is one strategy that works for them (but not everyone).

There is a difference between attainment and achievement. A student who rarely writes yet thinks up a story and produces half a page of work, has achieved something special whatever 'attainment figure' used. By encouraging students to develop independent thinking in assessing their own efforts, they gain an important tool for self-improvement.

Application

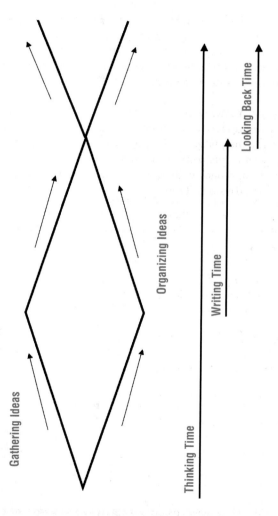

The creative writing process

Concept

Two key review questions

The writer Arthur C. Clarke asserts that a story is never actually finished, but only ever abandoned. In other words, the law of diminishing returns comes increasingly into play. Time constraints, and the fact that other projects are waiting in the wings, means that at some point we let go of the piece we've been working on and have done with it. Professionalism and perfectionism should never be confused. A writer's attitude to the work is his professionalism, where we do our best in the knowledge that everything we do is part of the learning journey.

The two review questions opposite are especially powerful. They presuppose a willingness to learn and improve and embody the realization that even recognized mistakes have the same learning value as things we feel we've done really well. To approach writing in this way establishes a very positive ethos over time.

Application

1. What changes do I need to make to this work for it to be the best I can do today?

2. What have I learned by doing this writing that will make my next piece of work even better?

Concept

Reaching for the right words

The American author Harlan Ellison was once asked during a radio interview how much he wrote each day. He replied 'Five hundred words.' The show's host tactlessly mentioned that this didn't seem much for a day's work. An icy silence ensued, followed by Ellison's withering response... 'Yes, but they're the *right* five hundred words each day.'

I think this is a key point. Even during the flow of composition, control of the language is vital. Sheer experience of language will boost the vocabulary and develop a sense of which words 'feel' right. Reaching for the right words – that is, the words that most vividly convey what we're thinking – is as much of an intuitive process as it is an intellectual one. Reflecting during the review phase further refines the communicative power of the writing.

Application

Here's a brief extract from a short story. Have students read through it and suggest improvements based on the notion of 'the right words for the right job'.

By a ray of pale white moonlight Eleanor saw the shadows getting nearer. They came snaking, sneaking, curling, crawling, jumping, dancing out from among the trees like the great unfolding of a wizard's gowns. They swept across the open space and left patches of dead grass behind. They swooped up to treetop height then sank low as an old man's bowed back. They twirled around and within and among themselves and became an old woman's tatters, slung about old shoulders.

She looked to be as ancient as rock, this stranger. She was stooped with the weight of many years or many sins, Eleanor did not know which. Her eyes were glaring in their knowingness. They could read anything as easily as reading a book. But beyond that the woman was elusive and Eleanor couldn't decide if she was heart-stoppingly ugly or breathtakingly beautiful. It all depended upon the way you looked at her. She smiled, crone and queen, and Eleanor felt a terrible ache as though she was suddenly home.

"I'm – "

"I know who you are." The voice was like the crackling of glass. "I am Tuggie Bannock. You know me."

Eleanor shook her head.

"Oh yes you do. Everybody knows me, sooner or later. I am the truth that comes back. I am the balance that makes the world fair. I am the sister who will not cast the first stone."

"I don't know what you mean." Eleanor's heart was pounding. She did know. Of course she knew! But things like this didn't happen. Why her? What had she done?

Concept

Review stars

The 'six big important questions', where, when, who, why, what, how (see also p22) can be used effectively at the review stage of writing. Rather than blanket-marking students' work, simply read it through and put a star or two in the margin at places where the narrative is vague or lacking in detail. Then encourage the students to focus on those scenes and ask as many of the six questions as are appropriate...

- Where does this scene happen? (Is there enough descriptive detail of place?)

- When does this event occur? (Does there need to be a time reference here?)

- Who should be here? (Have I forgotten any characters? Where should all of my characters be now?)

- Why do my characters choose those words? (Can my dialogue be crisper, briefer, more powerful?)

- What else could I include or leave out at this point?

- How would the scene develop most naturally?

Application

Here is the original version of the extract used on p89. Have students review it and ask some or all of the questions opposite.

By a gleam of pale moonlight Eleanor saw the shadows advancing. They came snaking, sneaking, curling, crawling out from among the maples like the great unfolding of a wizard's robes. They swept across the open space and left a swathe of dead grass behind. They swooped up to treetop height then sank low as a slave's bowed back. They twirled around and within and among themselves and became an old woman's tatters, slung about bony shoulders.

She looked to be as ancient as rock, this stranger. She was stooped with the weight of many years or many sins, Eleanor did not know which. Her eyes were powerful in their knowingness. They could read anything. But beyond that the woman was elusive and Eleanor couldn't decide if she was heart-stoppingly ugly or breathtakingly beautiful. It all depended upon the way you looked at her. She smiled, crone and queen, and Eleanor felt a terrible ache as though she was suddenly home.

"I'm – "

"I know who you are." The voice was like the crackling of sticks. "I am Tuggie Bannock. You know me."

Eleanor shook her head.

"Oh yes you do. Everybody knows me, sooner or later. I am the truth that comes back. I am the balance that makes the world fair. I am the sister who will not cast the first stone."

"I don't know what you mean." Eleanor's heart was pounding. She did know. Of course she knew! But things like this didn't happen. Why her? What had she done?

Concept

Four areas for review

The four areas are –

1. Mastery of conventions. How familiar is the writer with the motifs and typical stylistic features of the genre?

2. Affective responses. What emotional responses did the writer intend and how far have these been achieved?

3. Vivid details (even in more objective, scientific, 'intellectual' writing). What descriptive details are present that evoke vivid imagery and draw an emotional response?

4. Technical aspects. These include the conventions of the form the writing takes, grammar, punctuation, syntax, and so on.

The vocabulary can be changed for younger writers thus:

1. What kind of story?

2. Clear details.

3. How does the reader feel?

4. Choosing the right words.

Application

You may wish to use the 1–6 'hierarchy of understanding' scale, below, to evaluate the four areas for review. This is a tool that students can also use during their own reviews.

1	I don't understand this idea and I haven't tried to use it.
2	I think I understand this idea and I've tried to use it.
3	I do understand this idea and I can show someone else how to use it.
4	I have used / will use this idea in other kinds of writing.
5	I know how to apply this idea in other subject areas.
6	I know how to explain this idea in my own words and use it in a wide range of situations.

1–6 'hierarchy of understanding' scale

Pages 94–95 show an example of how the four areas for review can be broken down into smaller components.

Concept

Writer's pie

This technique looks in more detail at the four areas for review (see p92).

- Use a template such as the top one on p95.

- Identify the aspects of the student's work to be reviewed – those in the template are suggestions.

- Use the 1–6 scale as a guide.

- Make a mark in each slice of the pie (see the worked example) corresponding to the number selected from the 1–6 scale. The position of the stars shows where the student is on the scale: near the centre = 1; near the outer edge = 6.

> **TIP:**
> Keep these assessments and on a future occasion have students review the same aspects of their work. In many cases they will see very graphically that they have improved on many fronts.

Application

Writer's pie

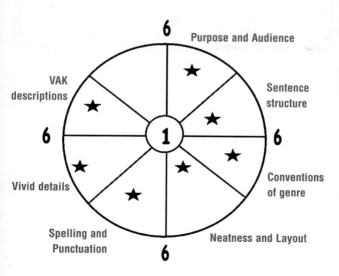

Writer's pie – worked example

References

Bowkett, Stephen (2001) *ALPS StoryMaker*, Network Educational Press
The *ALPS StoryMaker* pack uses fiction to develop creativity and thinking. The focus is creative writing, but the emerging thinking skills are applicable across the curriculum. The teacher's manual links theory with up to a hundred techniques that can be used across a wide age and ability range. This is complemented by a fiction resource – three books of short stories – and a CD of interactive games and audio files.

Bowkett, Stephen (2003) *StoryMaker Catch Pack*, Network Educational Press
This pack extends the *ALPS StoryMaker* resource. Again there is a teacher's manual, CD and three books of short stories. The focus is Science Fiction, Fantasy and Horror.

Bowkett, Stephen (2005) *100 Ideas for Teaching Creativity*, Continuum

Bowkett, Stephen (2006) *100 Ideas for Teaching Thinking Skills*, Continuum

Brownjohn, Sandy (1986) *Does It Have To Rhyme?*, Hodder & Stoughton

Brownjohn, Sandy (1993) *The Ability To Name Cats*, Hodder & Stoughton

Brownjohn, Sandy with Whitaker, Janet (1998) *Word Games*, Hodder & Stoughton

Bryson, Bill (1991) *Mother Tongue*, Penguin Books

Claxton, Guy (1998) *Hare Brain Tortoise Mind*, Fourth Estate

Fogarty, Robin and Bellanca, James (1986) *Teach Them Thinking*, Skylight

Gardner, Howard (1993) *Multiple Intelligences: The Theory in Practice*, Basic Books

Jackson, Steve and Livingstone, Ian (2002; originally published by Penguin in 1982) *The Warlock of Firetop Mountain*, Wizard Books

Leat, David and Nicols, Adam (1999) *Theory into Practice: mysteries make you think*, The Geographical Association

Postman, Neil and Weingartner, Charles (1972) *Teaching as a Subversive Activity*, Penguin Education

Propp, Vladimir (2001) *Morphology of the Folktale*, University of Texas Press

Rockett, Mel and Percival, Simon (2002) *Thinking for Learning*, Network Educational Press

Sedgewick, Fred (2003) *Teaching Poetry*, Classmates series, Continuum

Coptic Life
in
Egypt

T5-ARH-888

WITHDRAWN

The Catholic
Theological Union
LIBRARY
Chicago, Ill.

Coptic Life in Egypt

Claudia
Yvonne
Wiens

Introduced by
Yousriya Loza Sawiris

The Catholic
Theological Union
LIBRARY
Chicago, Ill.

The American University in Cairo Press
Cairo   New York

This project was made possible
by the generous sponsorship of
Naguib Sawiris

Copyright © 2003 by
The American University in Cairo Press
113 Sharia Kasr el Aini, Cairo, Egypt
420 Fifth Avenue, New York, NY 10018
www.aucpress.com

All rights reserved. No part of this
publication may be reproduced, stored
in a retrieval system or transmitted in
any form or by any means, electronic,
mechanical, photocopying, recording or
otherwise, without the prior written
permission of the publisher.

Dar el Kutub No. 19214/02
ISBN 977 424 786 8

Designed by
Andrea El-Akshar/AUC Press Design Center
Printed in Egypt

Introduction

by Yousriya Loza Sawiris

The Copts, the native Christians of Egypt, regard their country as especially blessed, being the only place outside the Holy Land where Jesus Christ set foot, when the Holy Family spent three years here to escape the persecution of Herod. And the Copts proudly trace their faith and their church to the arrival at Alexandria of St. Mark the Apostle, who brought with him firsthand the mass celebrated by Christ—this mass, translated into Coptic, was later collected and organized into the first recorded liturgy by Cyril I, the 24th patriarch of the Coptic Church. The faith of the early Coptic martyrs was an inspiration to Christians everywhere. Egypt was also the birthplace of Christian monasticism, following the example of St. Antony in the Eastern Desert in the fourth century, and the Catechetical School of Alexandria was a leading light in the development of thought and the defense of faith in the early Christian church. Today's Copts remain firm in their faith and proud of their heritage, which has made such vital contributions to Christianity as a whole.

This book describes and illustrates in words and pictures the life of the Copts in Egypt from a foreign visitor's point of view: how they practice their religion, how they keep old traditions alive, and how this is reflected in their everyday life, in such forms as *mulids*—celebrations of the birthdays or martyrdom of saints that are attended by thousands of people, both Christian and Muslim. The photographer also examines the life of Egypt's garbage collectors, the *zabbalin*—both Christians and Muslims working in the same trade—and describes their work and what a great difference the promotion of their basic needs—housing, schools, health care—through governmental and non-governmental social programs has made to their lives and to their children's futures.

The Coptic pope, His Holiness Shenouda III, maintains a close contact with his people through his weekly public meetings held every Wednesday, which hundreds of Copts attend, and his closeness and accessibility clearly have a deep influence on how the Copts live and practice their religion.

I appreciate the work Claudia Wiens has done in photographing and writing this book, and I hope it will help people—especially Egyptians—to understand and appreciate some aspects of our life in Egypt.

Acknowledgments

The photographs in this book were taken between February and October 2001 during my extended travels in Egypt. I spent a lot of time researching the right places and the right time to visit. *Coptic Egypt* by Jill Kamil (AUC Press, 1990) and *Two Thousand Years of Coptic Christianity* by Otto F.A. Meinardus (AUC Press, 1999) were a great help in my research and in my understanding of customs and traditions related to historical backgrounds. The rest of 2001 I spent selecting from more than 1,500 photographs. I would like to thank Heiner Schmitz and Axel Wehrtmann, who both helped me a lot to separate the wheat from the chaff and to put my photographs in the right order. This also gives me the opportunity to thank other people whose help, at one time or another, is reflected in the outcome of this book, namely Manon Atta, Dominic Coldwell, Eli Farinha, Kees Hulsmann, Hendrik Mallmann, Sabine Scheer, Antje Schimpf, and René Wenzel/designbureau martin & wenzel, Leyla, and my mother.

Above all, I owe a great debt to all Copts who provided me with necessary information concerning when and where to go, to all who appear in my photographs, and to all who helped me to overcome expected and unexpected obstacles.

Finally I want to thank all the people who constantly supported and encouraged me to go on when I was about to give up because the way seemed so long and stony.

This project gave me a great opportunity to see different sides and sites of Egypt that I otherwise would never have made the effort to explore.

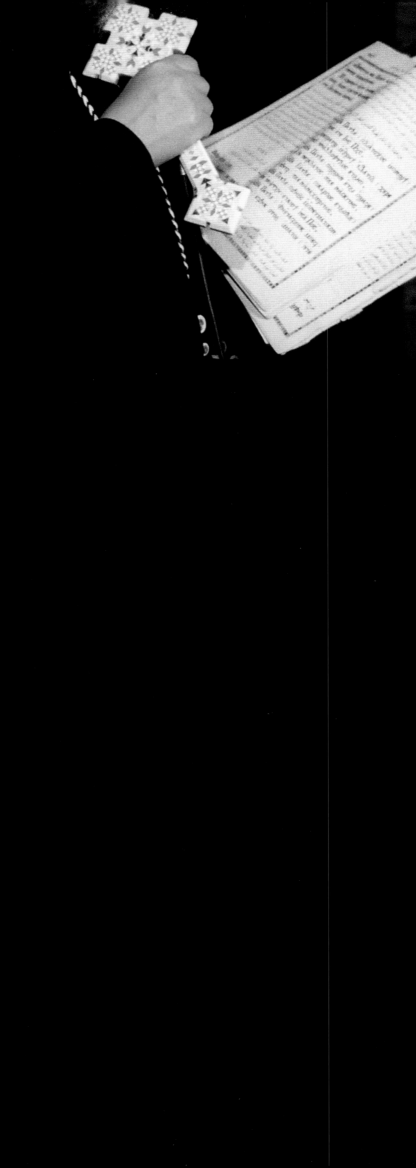

The Beginning of Christianity in Egypt

And when they were departed, behold, the angel of the Lord appeareth to Joseph in a dream, saying, Arise, and take the young child and his mother, and flee into Egypt, and be thou there until I bring thee word: for Herod will seek the young child to destroy him. (Matt. 2:13–15)

Thus began the flight of the Holy Family (including Salomé, the nanny) from Bethlehem to Egypt. The present literature differs as to the exact route the family took, because few written testimonies are extant. Experts agree, however, that the Family probably moved through Faras, Galilea, and Beersheva in present-day Israel, and from there entered Egypt, stopping in Tell al-Farama, Tell Basta, Musturud, Bilbays, Sammanud, al-Burullus, Sakha, Wadi al-Natrun, al-Qanatir, al-Matariya, Harat Zuwayla, Old Cairo, Maadi, Bahnasa, Gebel al-Tayr, Ashmunayn, Mallawi, Kom Maria, Dayrut, Qusiya, Mir, and Qusqam.

Although the exact duration of the Family's stay is not clear either, most sources speak of a period of between three and a half and four years.

During the journey, the young Jesus is said to have performed various miracles, curing the sick, resurrecting a number of people from death, and drawing water from the ground during periods of drought and famine.

Every time the Holy Family entered a temple, it is reported that the statues of pagan deities would collapse and shatter. Various sites on the Family's itinerary still feature churches and other sacred sites, including the monasteries of Deir al-Suryan, Deir Anba Bishoi, Deir Abu Maqar, and Deir al-Baramus in Wadi Natrun, Deir Abu Hinnis in Mallawi, and Deir al-Muharraq in Qusqam.

The Holy Family probably took the same route when they returned to Palestine, and it is reported that during their stay at a place where the Monastery of the Holy Virgin now stands, an angel of the Lord appeared to Joseph in a dream,

> Saying, Arise, and take the young child and his mother, and go into the land of Israel: for they are dead which sought the young child's life. (Matt. 2:20)

St. Mark the Evangelist first introduced Christianity to Egypt in the first century AD during the reign of the Roman emperor Claudius. Although no source mentions the exact dates of his visits, it is likely that he was in Egypt in AD 41/42 or perhaps 43/44, and perhaps again between 50 and 62. He was definitely there in 68, the year of his martyrdom.

St. Mark not only authored the oldest canonical Gospel, but also founded the Coptic Church. He was the first in an unbroken chain of 117 Coptic patriarchs. Legend has it that his first Egyptian convert was a cobbler in Alexandria. St. Mark converted and baptized the cobbler's entire family. Soon, the number of converts increased. At the same time, there were growing fears that Christians would outnumber the followers of the old gods. St. Mark was therefore imprisoned on Easter Sunday in 68. An angel appeared, promising him the crown of martyrdom. And so it happened. The following day, St. Mark was tortured and dragged through the streets of Alexandria until he died. That night, his disciples gathered to bury him in the church.

Despite persecution, Christianity quickly penetrated to the south, into Upper Egypt, because the spiritual climate of Egypt offered a ready basis for Christian belief. In part, Egyptians welcomed Christianity because of similarities with much older religious traditions. The popularity of the Virgin Mary undoubtedly stems from the similarity of her story to the myth of Isis, the pharaonic mother-goddess who protected her child, Horus, from enemies. The places where the Holy Family rested became hallowed sites.

Religion in Daily Life

People in Egypt like to exhibit their religious beliefs. In every store, juice bar, ironing shop, or commercial establishment run by Copts, tokens of Christianity are on display. Stickers of saints are stuck to walls and crosses decorate rooms. Even taxi drivers embellish their cars with stickers of Jesus and the saints. Muslims do not show pictures because Islam frowns on depictions of God or the Prophet, but they do use embellished script like "Allahu Akbar" (God is Great) to demonstrate their piety. Egyptians are proud of their religion and define themselves through it.

Every Wednesday evening, thousands of listeners flock to St. Mark's Cathedral in the district of Abbasiya to attend a two-hour sermon headed by the Coptic pope Shenouda III. Members of the audience write down questions, which are collected before the sermon gets under way. First, Pope Shenouda signs posters and books. He then talks about a recent religious event or problem and, finally, he reads out the questions and answers them. This weekly event contributes to a close relationship between the people and church. This is an attempt to make official religion more understandable for the ordinary people. The pope is a figurehead, but an accessible one, which makes it easy for people to identify with him.

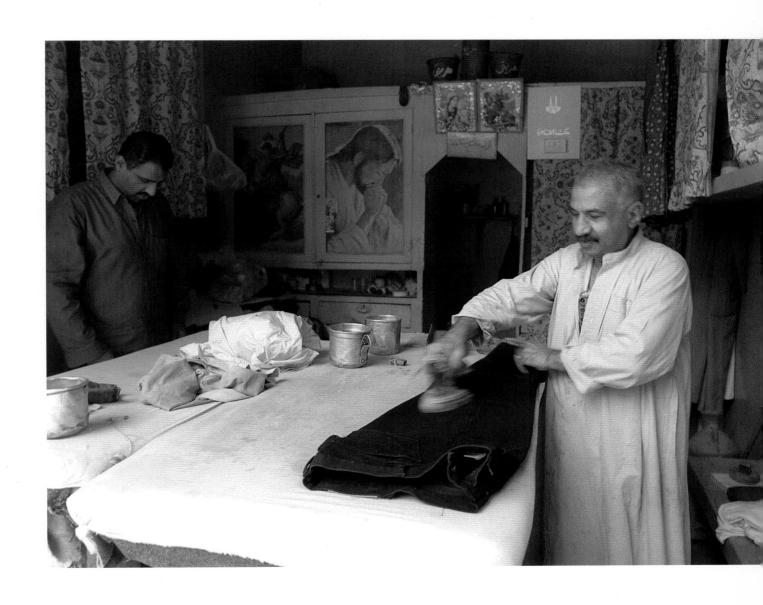

8

IN THE NAME OF THE LORD: TEACHER, REBUKE YOUR DISCIPLES. IF THEY KEEP QUIET THE STONES WILL CRY OUT!

The Muqattam
Community

The garbage collectors of Cairo—the *zabbalin*—are largely Copts. The *zabbalin* keep pigs because they consume organic waste, and it is because Muslims consider pigs to be impure animals that the job is done mainly by Copts. Many of them migrated a long time ago from rural areas to the capital in search of better employment prospects. When lucrative jobs failed to materialize, the migrants saw no other option but to join the swelling ranks of the city's garbage collectors. To improve hygienic conditions, the pig-keeping is beeing moved out of the populated areas of Cairo to areas outside the city.

For over fifty years the *zabbalin* have collected private and public garbage in Cairo. With small trucks or donkey carts, the men and boys drive from house to house in the early hours of the morning collecting garbage and transporting it to one of the five garbage areas in Cairo: Muqattam, Tura, Mu'tamadiya, Baragil, and Ezbit al-Nakhla. Altogether there are about 65,000 people in Cairo involved in garbage activities like collecting, sorting, and recycling. About 20,000 of them live in Muqattam, at the foot of the mountain of the same name, near the famous citadel. When the men come home in the morning with the garbage, the sorting work begins for the women and children. They divide it into heaps of glass, paper, metal for recycling, and into another pile of organic waste for pig food. The non-organic waste is sold to recycling plants.

The inhabitants of these areas live under difficult conditions, but these have been improved during the last few years by the efforts of NGOs and the government. Now there is drinking water, electricity, and a functioning sewage system, and the medical care has improved a great deal. In Muqattam there are several elementary schools and also secondary schools. The NGOs offer additional reading and writing courses, some specifically for women and children. There are also several kindergartens and clubs for children. Medical care is provided by the medical centers of NGOs, a monastery hospital, and a clinic established by H.E. Mrs. Suzanne Mubarak.

Eighty-five percent of collected garbage gets recycled. This activity creates workplaces, is positive for the environment (because less garbage must be stored or burned), and is also good for the economy (because less raw materials have to be bought). In 1984, an NGO constructed a center in the middle of Muqattam. They established a children's club, a recycling place for paper and cloth, and, in addition, they offer classes in the prevention of hepatitis and other issues. Using recycled paper and cloth, the women produce postcards, carpets, and other saleable items. They receive an education and earn their own money.

In spite of their poverty, or perhaps because of their poverty, the garbage collectors retain a strong faith in religion. The piety of the Copts fuelled a strong desire to build a church in Muqattam. While searching for a proper location, they chanced upon a cavernous excavation in the mountain. With the help of donations and much personal commitment, they erected a church here, which they named after St. Samaan the shoemaker. Legend has it that St. Samaan moved the Muqattam Mountain in AD 979—proving Jesus' dictum, "If ye have faith as a grain of mustard seed, ye shall say unto this mountain, Remove hence to yonder place; and it shall remove; and nothing shall be impossible unto you" (Matt. 17:20).

In 1977, Pope Shenouda III visited and blessed the church for the first time. Since then he has visited regularly, and four more churches and a monastery have been built in the same area. The whole complex is financed by donations from visitors. There is a spacious picnic area attached to the complex, where visitors can combine religious contemplation with mundane recreation in a way that narrows the gap between the poor and the institution of the Church.

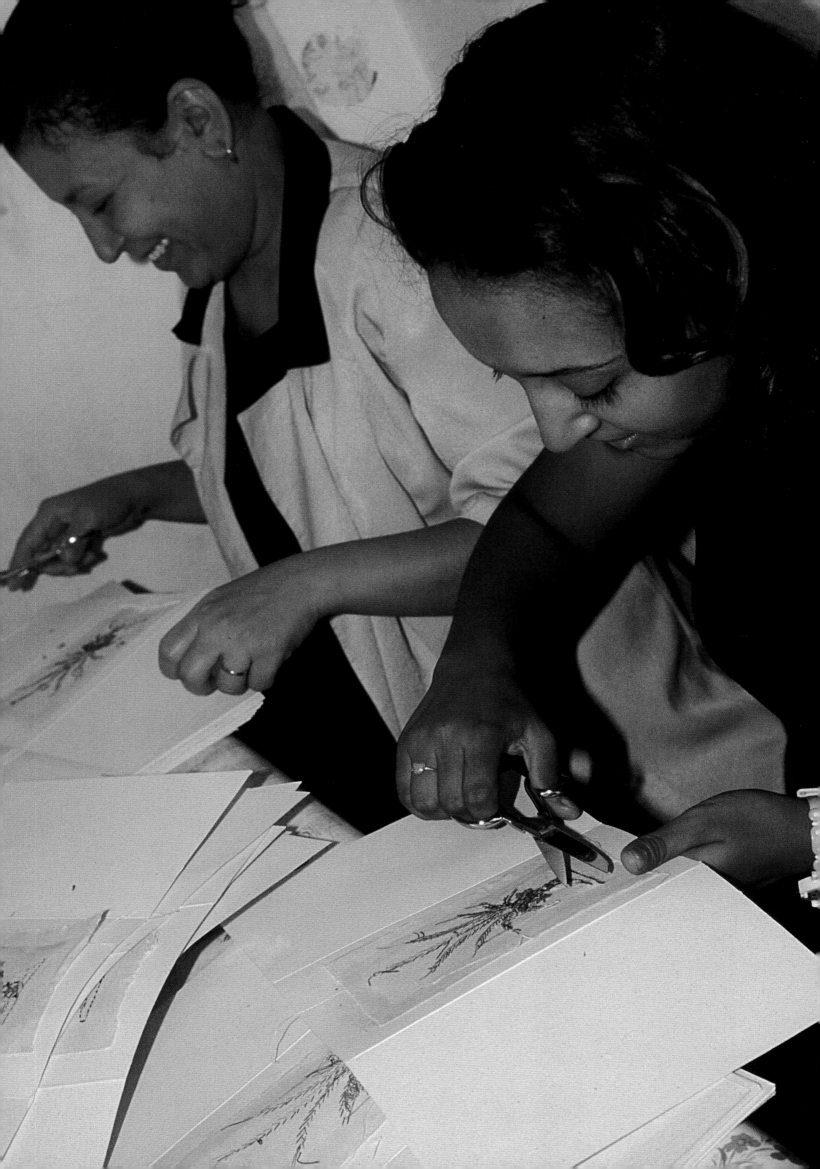

Mulids and Pilgrimages

*M*ulids, 'birthdays' of saints, martyrs, and holy men, are cele-brated in Egypt by both Muslims and Copts. Christian *mulids* are celebrated by many people as annual pilgrimages. *Mulids* belong to the folk religion, which includes many aspects of personal and social life. The religious attitude and traditions of the masses differ greatly from the attitude and traditions of the official church, although there are some overlaps. Most of the rit-uals of the folk religion have their roots in the religious heritage of pharaonic Egypt. The religious attitude of Egyptians has always been determined by eschatology, a factor that doubtlessly eased the acceptance of Christianity. Copts believed that people were living for their reception in paradise, and they therefore received the death of a saint or a martyr as a birthday. Only in the fourth century was it transformed into a burial. Until modern times, Copts see the saint's martyrdom as a 'second birth' into Eternal Life. Many people continued to follow the traditions of their pharaonic ancestors, and pharaonic deities were replaced by saints and martyrs, who became objects of veneration and wor-ship. After a short time every settlement had its own patron saints and martyrs, for whom shrines and tombs were erected in which their bones were kept as objects of veneration and prayer. Every saint and martyr was related to miraculous stories that suited their martyrdom. Saints and martyrs were a more tangible and real object of religious identification than the abstract dogmas of the official religion.

Soon there were annual *mulids* at the tombs and shrines of saints. These took place in monasteries and churches and other holy sites. An important aspect of a *mulid* is the miraculous events that are related to it. These phenomena have a long-standing history and are expected to happen regularly. They are the divine proof of the holiness of the feast.

These miracles are of two types. There are those that pertain to single individuals, such as the granting of fertility to sterile women, the curing of mentally or emotionally sick people, exorcism, or the restoration of lost or stolen belongings. And there are the apparitions, such as lights or the shape of the Holy Virgin in form of a bright light, as occurred several times in August 2000 at St. Mark's church in Asyut. The lights came as a series between the church towers and they came together to form the shape of the Virgin Mary. Many believers testify that they have seen apparitions at holy sites. Many mentally or emotionally sick people, sterile women, and other pilgrims attend *mulids* hoping to be healed or blessed.

Most *mulids* are not only serious events but also occasions of much fun and joy. The annual ten-day *mulid* at Deir al-Muharraq in Middle Egypt resembles a huge picnic or a funfair. The music is loud, people dance, and there are merchants selling kitschy Taiwanese items, nuts, fruits, and pictures of saints. Not to be missed are the tattoo artists who tattoo the Coptic cross onto the wrists of Copts. They also draw bigger pictures of saints on arms and shoulders. It is estimated that 50,000 people make the pilgrimage to Deir al-Muharraq every year. For the poor among the Copts, which is a high percentage of the Copts in Middle Egypt, a *mulid* is often the only holiday they can afford. They pitch their tents around the monastery for several days and visit the churches to pray, say intercessions, and touch shrines and pictures of saints and martyrs in order to attain cure and blessings. Many families bring sheep and goats as sacrifices. These are slaughtered in the monastery's butchery, blessed by a priest or monk, and then shared.

A *mulid* is also a good occasion for baptizing babies. It is common for the monks to baptize several hundred babies during a *mulid* that lasts a few days. Baptism is the first and most important sacrament, and without it, no other sacrament can be administered; it is a prerequisite for salvation and entry into the kingdom of God, according to Jesus' words: "Except a man be born of water and of the Spirit, he cannot enter into the kingdom of God" (John 3:5). Baptism is the sacrament in which the recipient is regenerated through triple immersion into water in the name of the Father, the Son, and the Holy Spirit and thus united with Christ and the body of the Church. Babies should be baptized as soon as possible once they are eighty days old (for girls) or forty days old (for boys), the prescribed periods of time after giving birth that a woman is considered impure and is not allowed to participate in religious acts such as Holy Communion or Baptism. In cases of illness, or if there is a fear that the baby might not survive this period, somebody else can take it to church. After the baby has been immersed three times he or she then receives thirty-two crosses of oil on the skin.

Copts venerate many martyrs but only a few saints. The Holy Virgin holds the strongest position and receives the most veneration. Thirty-two celebrations are held each year in her honor.

Another reason for pilgrimages is the long and persistent tradition that supports the Bible story of the Holy Family's flight into Egypt (Matt. 2:13–15). Many feasts take place at the sites where the Holy Family are believed to have rested during their flight. One of these commemorations takes place every June 1 in the area of Deir Abu Hinnis in Middle Egypt. The bishop of Mallawi, two other bishops, and several clerical dignitaries cross the Nile in a splendidly decorated sailing boat. The crossing symbolizes the trip of the Holy Family on the Nile. Thousands of believers follow the sailing boat to the other river bank. From there a procession goes to the peak of Mount Kom Maria, singing joyful sacred songs and passing churches and Deir Abu Hinnis along the way. Kom Maria is famous for granting fertility to sterile women. Now and then one can see a woman rolling down the mountain praying for fertility. On the top of the mountain a tent is pitched for the clerical dignitaries and servants who commemorate the visit of the Holy Family to this area. A ceremony with singing children and speeches lasts a couple of hours. Thousands of pilgrims assemble outside the festivity tent to take part in the commemoration celebration.

Another feast in honor of the Holy Family and especially of the Holy Virgin is held at the Holy Virgin Mary Church on Gebel al-Tayr (Mountain of Birds) in Middle Egypt. According to tradition this is the site where Mary feared for Jesus' safety because a huge rock threatened to fall down on them. But Jesus extended his hand and kept the rock away. It is said that Jesus left the imprint of his hand behind. Pilgrims come from near and far, cross the Nile, and gather in a joyful procession with singing and drumming.

Another *mulid*, which lasts fifteen days and which is very crowded, takes place in August at Deir al-Adra (Monastery of the Holy Virgin) in Durunka, 10 kilometers from Asyut. A huge funfair (there is even a merry-go-round) is located at the bottom of the hill. In August 2001 the *mulid* attracted more than 20,000 people because of light apparitions on several evenings. The believers were convinced that heaven was talking to the people.

51

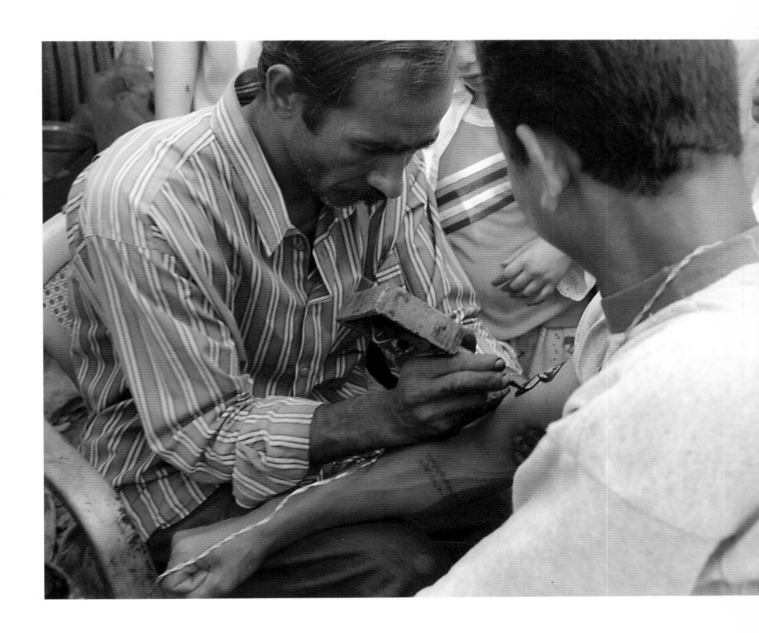

 72

The Sacrament
of Marriage

The Coptic wedding is also called the 'Coronation Ceremony' because the priest crowns the couple for a short while during the ceremony. Normally, the wedding takes place after an extended period of engagement, in which the couple gets to know each other better. This also holds true for arranged marriages, which are still quite common. The wedding usually takes place in a church—it is only under exceptional circumstances now that the wedding is held at home, but only a few decades ago it was customary to celebrate the marriage at the groom's house.

The bride and the groom are accompanied separately to the church, which is decorated with flowers. They sit on gilded chairs on a small dais. Facing the couple is a table that carries the New Testament, a golden cross, the wedding rings, and incense. The clergy are dressed in festive habits and accompany the ceremony with joyful chants and the sound of cymbals. The priest anoints the couple's wrists and foreheads with sacred oil. Afterwards he briefly places the crowns, which bear a Coptic cross inscribed with the phrase "Glory to God in the highest and on earth peace," on their heads. The priest utters the words "Crown them with glory and honor, O Father, Amen. Bless them, O only begotten Son, Amen. Sanctify them, O Holy Spirit, Amen." The couple exchange rings; the priest reads verses from the Bible, and, at the end, the congregation recites a prayer.

Wedding parties are held at home, in hotels, or at clubs according to the families' financial circumstances. Coptic couples usually marry for life. Only under exceptional circumstances, such as adultery or a spouse's conversion to Islam, is divorce acceptable.

Pages 78–85:

Wedding ceremony in

a church in Shubra

Monastic Life

In the third century, thousands of ascetics started to live alone or in small groups separated from the secular world. Inspired by the example of the Desert Fathers Paul and Antony, many hermits found the solitude that they desired deep in the desert. St. Paul (228–343) and St. Antony (251–356) lived in complete solitude in the desert west of the Red Sea. Their lives were filled with meditation and prayer. Because of this ascetic way of living, they became spiritual leaders and the founders of the monastic lifestyle. Thousands of people followed their example. St. Antony presented two principles, which appeared to him in an apparition, to his followers: work and prayer. In addition, he introduced the monastic garb, a garment of flax fastened by a leather belt, and a sheepskin cloak for colder days.

Most of the hermits lived in caves and came together only on Saturdays and Sundays for spiritual guidance. Ascetic leaders were often from simple origins, like St. Paul, but also from higher social classes, like St. Antony. When rich landowners decided to abandon their worldly possessions to become hermits, they received special respect and were regarded as having a certain spiritual power and a close relationship with the divine. The Desert Fathers became heroes to whom a divine power was attributed.

In the fourth century, shortly after St. Antony's death, Deir Anba Antunyus was built in his honor close to the cave where he had spent his life. The monastery of Deir Anba Bula was founded not far from Deir Anba Antunyus at the end of the fifth or the beginning of the sixth century in honor of St. Paul. Nowadays, both monasteries celebrate the anniversaries of the two saints. The monks of the one monastery always come to join the feast of the other. The feast of St. Paul is held in the old underground church where his remains are buried. The monks play music and sing songs that tell the story of Paul. Later in the evening a procession through the monastery's courtyard takes place. Thousands of believers, who come especially for this event, wait to touch pictures of St. Paul to receive blessings.

As Islam spread and Christianity declined over the centuries, many monasteries lost their popularity. A Christian revival began only in the nineteenth century. It gathered force in the 1940s with the birth of the Sunday School movement. Nowadays, Pope Shenouda III, head of Egypt's Orthodox Church, supports church festivals, Coptic liturgical studies, and other church activities to awaken the interest of the youth in religion and the church. Young people can try monastic life during their school holidays. Over the last fifty years, the number of monks has increased from about 200 to almost 2,000. Also, the number of applicants for the priesthood and for convents has gone up. The reasons for this increase are not clear. Many Copts attribute the church's popularity to the growth of a powerful Christian youth movement. Others say that young people find many roads closed, but that they need to express themselves, and that they find this possible in monasteries and churches.

The monastic lifestyle is modest and daily life revolves around work, prayer, and meditation. Food is simple and consists mainly of bread, beans, and other vegetables. Many monasteries aim for self-reliance. They rent land to farmers in order to earn money, or they sell their own produce. Deir Abu Mina, near Alexandria, is one of the richest monasteries in Egypt. It supports itself through fish and chicken farming, the cultivation of olives and vegetables, and renting land to farmers, and it even has its own microchip laboratory. The monasteries of Middle Egypt, such as Deir al-Muharraq are also wealthy.

Pages 89–91:
Deir Anba Bishoi, Wadi Natrun

Pages 92–93:
Deir Anba Bula

Pages 94–107:
Feast honoring St. Paul at Deir Anba Bula; monks from Deir Anba Bula and their guests from Deir Anba Antunyus celebrate together

Easter

Easter is the most important Coptic holiday. It surpasses Christmas both in importance and in the scope of celebrations. Because the Coptic calendar differs from the western one, Easter generally is celebrated later than in the west.

Copts fast 55 rather than 40 days before Easter. In the Coptic tradition, the faithful refrain from eating animal products such as meat, eggs, milk, and fish. Copts also need to abstain from drinking coffee and alcohol during the fast. Just like Muslims during the holy month of Ramadan, they may only eat between sunset and sunrise. Children, pregnant women, the elderly, and the sick are excused from the fast.

The Holy Easter week, *Usbu' al-Alam* (Week of Pain), is a period of prayer and contemplation commemorating Jesus' last days on earth. It starts with Palm Sunday *(Ahad al-Za'f)* and finishes on Easter Sunday. On Palm Sunday, people visit their relatives' graves and remember the dead. Priests conduct mass in church and lead processions carrying palm leaves woven in the shape of crosses. They also swing incense burners. Outside church, artisans plait palm leaves and sell them to people to hang over the front doors of their houses to ward off evil spirits. On Thursday, Copts commemorate Christ washing the feet of the disciples. On Good Friday *(al-Gum'a al-Hazina)* the altars are draped with black sheets to mourn Jesus' crucifixion. Good Saturday is called the Saturday of Light *(Sabt al-Nur)*, because of the miracle that reportedly illuminated the Holy Sepulcher in Jerusalem. Some locations also hold candlelight processions.

At midnight on Saturday, churches across the country hold mass. Pope Shenouda III conducts mass in St. Mark's Cathedral in Cairo.

Thousands of people come to the cathedral. Clerics dress in splendid robes. The pope himself wears an ornate robe and a crown.

The ceremony of opening the churches' inner sanctuary symbolically evokes the removal of the stone that sealed Jesus' grave. Processions led by a priest holding an icon of Jesus circumambulate the sanctuary.

The spectators attending mass get very excited when the pope passes by them to offer his blessings, not least because the papal benediction is thought to convey healing powers. The sermon is simultaneously translated into sign language. It ends, several hours later, with the Holy Communion.

Christmas celebrations resemble the festivities of the Easter season, but are smaller in scope. The Coptic Christmas is celebrated on January 7.

Pages 111–113:
Palm Sunday celebration at
St. Mary's Church in Maadi

Pages 114–125:
Easter celebration at St. Mark's
Cathedral in Abbasiya

Pages 115, 120, 122:
Pope Shenouda III

Page 126:
Shadows at Deir al-Adra at
Durunka

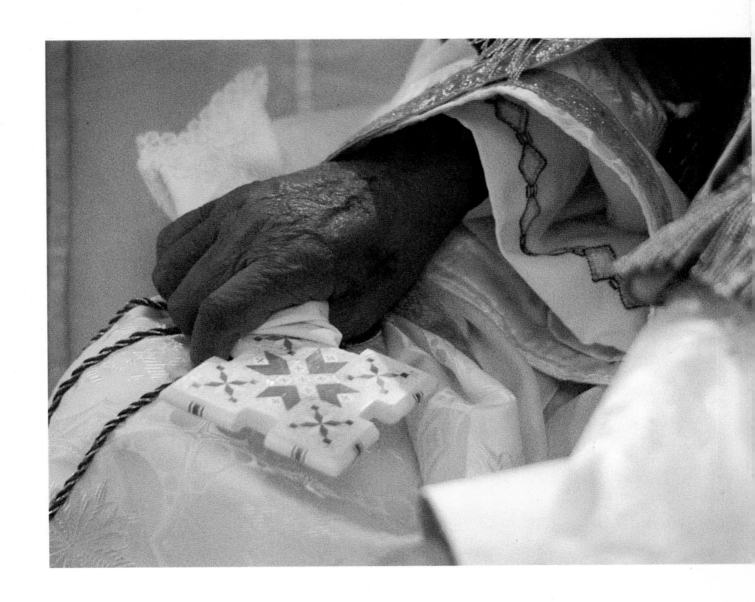

CATHOLIC THEOLOGICAL UNION

3 0311 00129 5802

WITHDRAWN

BX 134 .E4 W54 2003
Wiens, Claudia Yvonne.
Coptic life in Egypt

DEMCO